GROWING UP
Reading

Copyright © 1993 by Jill Frankel Hauser

Library of Congress
Cataloging-in-Publication Data

Hauser, Jill Frankel, 1950 –
    Growing up reading : learning to read through creative
play / Jill Frankel Hauser
    p.   cm.
ISBN 0–913589–73–X
    1. Reading (Early childhood)—United States.
    2. Reading—United States—Parent participation.
    3. Early childhood education—United States—Activity
programs.   4. Play — United States.   I. Title
LB1139.5.R43H38   1993
372.4—dc20   93-19175   CIP

Cover and interior design: Trezzo-Braren Studio
Printing: Capital City Press
Photography: Randall Hauser

Williamson Publishing Co.
P.O. Box 185
Charlotte, Vermont 05445
1-800-234-8791

Manufactured in the United States of America

10 9 8 7 6 5 4 3 2 1

Portions of this book were previously published in *Learning
and Loving to Read.*

Notice: The information contained in this book is true,
complete, and accurate to the best of our knowledge.
All recommendations and suggestions are made without
any guarantees on the part of the author or Williamson
Publishing. The author and publisher disclaim all liability
incurred in connection with the use of this information.

About the Author: Jill Frankel Hauser, M.A.,
Ed., is a recognized authority in the field of reading instruction. She brings to her first book more
than ten years of experience as a classroom
teacher, reading specialist, university instructor,
and teacher trainer.

In the classroom, clinic, and at home, her
techniques are both innovative and practical
and have been published nationally in journals
for educators and parents. She has also con-
ducted numerous workshops on reading instruction for parent and teacher groups.

Ms. Hauser firmly believes that the parent is
the child's most important teacher. Her child-
centered approach enables parents to create a
vital foundation of literacy skills and love of
reading to last a lifetime. Ms. Hauser's children
learned to read using the methods and activities
described in this book and read happily and
fluently before starting school.

A WILLIAMSON ⚘ KIDS LOVE TO LEARN BOOK

GROWING UP
Reading

LEARNING TO READ THROUGH CREATIVE PLAY

**FOR FUN-LOVING CHILDREN —
FROM EARLY MONTHS TO 7 YEARS
— AND THEIR BUSY PARENTS!**

JILL FRANKEL HAUSER

CONTENTS

DEDICATION

To the dauntless spirit of children to learn.

To Emunah, Savlan, and Zev, who inspired the book.

To Randy, who shared and supported the vision.

ACKNOWLEDGEMENTS

My deep appreciation goes to those parents, teachers, and friends whose infinitely valuable feedback and encouragement helped make this book possible: Molly Mancasola, Francie Parr, Debbie Spiess, Maxine and Melvin Frankel, Linda Fisher, The Staff of Shasta College Early Childhood Education Center, Quinby's Books of Redding, Cody's Books of Berkeley, Randy, Emunah, Savlan, and Zev Hauser.

I also wish to thank those families who let us photograph their precious children growing up reading: the Mancasola, Burk, Pry, Craig, Howard, Miramontes, Caldwell, Adkins, Smith, and Robidoux families.

Introduction

"Parents play rolls of inestimable importance in laying the foundation for learning to read. . . . Children who knew a lot about written language had parents who believed that it was their responsibility to seize opportunities to convey information about written language to children."

– Report of the Commission on Reading, National Academy of Education

You and your child are about to embark on an exciting, rewarding adventure. Soon, the print your child sees daily — from road signs to books — will have meaning. As this reading ability grows, your child's learning will soar, and the seeds will be planted for a lifelong love of reading.

You have already observed your child's remarkable drive to explore every facet of the environment. Print is part of this environment, and all forms of print can be fair game for discovery. It's as natural for children to make sense of print as it is for them to understand how snow feels or why a spider spins its web. A child digs in the sand, splashes in water, plays with toys — and reads — if given the right opportunities.

WHAT AN IDEAL TIME TO LEARN TO READ!

Research shows that a child's experiences at home during the preschool years set the stage for reading success. As a parent you are special. Your love for and understanding of your child make you his most effective first teacher. Because of this vital relationship, you can build on your child's interests and abilities, personalizing the learning experience. You are your child's best guide in unlocking the fascinating mystery of print. And your home, where your child has already succeeded in making so many interesting discoveries, is the perfect place to learn.

WHAT IDEAL COMPANY AND SURROUNDINGS FOR LEARNING TO READ!

Although most children have the capacity to learn to read, not all receive optimal opportunities for learning. My children learned to read when I combined two powerful resources: *the exceptional receptivity young children have toward learning, and the unique capacity parents have to influence that learning.* The opportunities I provided allowed my children to take the lead. By building on their interests and abilities, reading became very meaningful and important. In fact, they quickly became fluent readers through their own desire to find meaning in print.

With time being precious and children never in one place for long, mine learned to read right from their first day and throughout the many busy days that followed. Even as babies they heard the rhythmic language of nursery rhymes as I changed diapers. They chewed the corners of board books along with their exploration of other toys. As toddlers and preschoolers, they learned among cereal boxes in the shopping cart, while helping Dad sort garden seeds, and while listening to a bedtime story. When they asked, "What does that say?" or "How do I write . . .?" they were shown. I helped them make sense of print in the same way I explained any other aspect of the world that piqued their curiosity. Learning to read became part of their daily lives, and my children simply grew up reading. *Growing Up Reading* evolved from this experience. It will show you how to "seize opportunities," enabling your child to read while enriching the love and respect you share.

GUIDELINES FOR SUCCESS

Failure is impossible when a child's interests, abilities, and learning style lead the way. The closer you tailor the learning experience to the child, the more effective the learning will be. Here's how:

 ## ENCOURAGE PLAYFUL EXPLORATION

That's the natural way children learn. No rigid procedures or schedules are imposed. Instead, *Growing Up Reading* activities are adaptable to the unique interests and abilities of your child, while fitting in comfortably with the day. Whether you sample a few activities from time to time or try a wide variety, your child will grow up a stronger reader.

 ## MAKE SURE THE ACTIVITY IS APPROPRIATE

The most reliable indicator of an activity's appropriateness is the child's interest. Because children are natural learners, they are eager to learn skills relevant to their interests and challenging to their abilities. You know you've matched the activity to the child when the child becomes completely engaged in the process. Whether it's molding clay, tying a shoe, or reading a book, tune in to your child's level of enthusiasm. So how can you tell if an activity is appropriate for your child? Try it and see. Then let your child be the ultimate judge.

 ## ASSURE SUCCESS

Because success inspires learning, try activities that challenge without being too difficult. If your child finds an activity frustrating, boring, or "not fun," forget it for now. There are many more to try. Trust your intuition and respect your child's judgment. Pushing can jeopardize a child's precious natural love of learning.

 ## BE PATIENT

Have the expectation that your child will become an excellent reader and writer, but understand that learning to read, like all language skills, takes time. Children need freedom to explore and use as much written language as they like and at their own pace. Particular skills can take days, weeks, or months to master depending on a child's age, interests, abilities, and learning style. Respect that uniqueness and don't rush your child.

 ## APPRECIATE ALL EFFORT AND EXPLORATION

Complete the learning experience with plenty of hugs, kisses, joy, and enthusiasm.

When learning to read occurs with respect for the child, reading becomes a meaningful and joyous part of life.

HOW THIS BOOK IS ORGANIZED

Before you begin, familiarize yourself with the chapters and activity materials:

 THE PRINCIPLES, ESSENTIAL SKILLS, AND LEARNING ACTIVITIES

of *Growing Up Reading* are explained in the first eight chapters. Activities offered shape exploration for optimal learning.

 THE TREASURY FOR LITERACY INDEPENDENCE

is contained in chapter 9. It lists over 400 books and other resources to insure your child's smooth transition from beginning to independent reader. All books referred to throughout the book are referenced here.

 ACTIVITY MATERIALS

in this book are provided in appendix B. Most materials allow your child to touch and arrange letters, words, and pictures and are reusable for plenty of practice. Look for additional activities at the end of each chapter.

 FIRST READING BOOKS

are designed to be personalized to your child's interests and easily read. The books assure a successful first reading experience.

 SUGGESTIONS FOR EARLY CHILDHOOD EDUCATION PROGRAMS

are provided in appendix A. Ways are offered to transform any classroom or play area into a literary-rich environment.

The information in this book is presented in a purposeful order, one skill after another. But as you'll see, learning to read is a holistic process where different skills are learned concurrently. For example, children make first attempts to write at the same time they notice words in their environment, hear stories read aloud, enjoy books on their own, chant rhymes, and so on. Reading, writing, speaking, listening, and thinking are all interrelated. Skill in one area enhances skill in other areas. And reading itself requires simultaneous use of a variety of skills and strategies. Therefore, you'll be mixing activities from different chapters to offer simultaneous exploration of all aspects of literacy.

Although this book is written from the perspective of a parent and child, anyone who wishes to share the joy of reading with children will find it effective: grandparents, older siblings, care-givers, teachers, and day-care providers. And the activities can easily be adapted for use with small groups of children (see appendix A). Please note that pronoun gender (such as he or she) has been alternated chapter by chapter.

Reading

AN OVERVIEW OF THE DISCOVERY PROCESS

CHILDREN "READ" FROM BIRTH

Your child was "reading" as an infant at that magical moment he first responded to your smile. He found important meaning in your smile. And that's what reading is all about: *discovering meaning.* Reading written language is simply a process of discovering ideas from print.

From the first moment of consciousness children begin a relentless quest to make sense of their world. Along the way they learn to speak, not because they set out to, but because speech is a vital tool in helping them learn all they can. They also learn to read, if it, too, supports their learning quest.

Through my experience in the classroom, clinic, and at home, I've come to one fundamental conclusion: *Learning to read print must support the discovery process that begins at birth, expanding the child's growing knowledge of the world.* When this occurs, children learn with ease, becoming confident and enthusiastic readers. Indeed, they clearly excel in reading.

The discoveries children make fill them with ideas to communicate. They learn to talk in order to share their ideas and to listen in order to discover even more. When they understand that reading is also part of the discovery of ideas, they learn to read with equal ease and enthusiasm.

NATURAL LEARNING

Unfortunately, the goal of discovering meaning is often lost in traditional instructional methods. First children are taught letter sounds and to recognize isolated words on worksheets. Next they are taught comprehension skills. When they are finally offered a book they may wonder what it's for. Children who are taught with this approach may know *how* to read, but they probably won't.

Instead, reading instruction should follow the natural way children learn. We must instill a love and purpose for reading by offering them irresistible books and functional reading material right from the start. If children perceive that written language holds ideas vital to *their* interests, they will want to seek meaning from print. Then, growing from their desire to crack the print code, they will learn word recognition and phonics skills.

Reading is no more a process of pronouncing words, than listening is a process of hearing them. Instead, we seek ideas from both speech and print. Isolated skill drills and abstract fill-in-the-blank worksheets are tedious exercises that don't help children see reading as the discovery of ideas. Reading or listening to the reading of vital material does. If children are encouraged to learn about their interests by reading, they will learn to read almost effortlessly.

LIKE LEARNING TO SPEAK

Children can read and write as fluently as they speak — if they learn literacy in the same way they so successfully and effortlessly learned speech. Here's how children learn to speak followed by a sampling of ways that can be effectively applied to learning literacy. These methods will be discussed in depth in the rest of the chapters of this book.

 TOTAL IMMERSION

Let children experience books read aloud; signs and labels in our environment; a library full of books, magazines, catalogs; tools of the trade such as pencils, pens, and paper.

 SOCIAL INTERACTION WITH PARENTS

Model the use of written language in all ways and forms. Talk together about newly discovered ideas from books. The greater the interaction, the more effective the learning.

 LANGUAGE HELPS CHILDREN LEARN ABOUT THE WORLD

Offer irresistible reading material targeted to the child's own interests.

 LANGUAGE IS FRIENDLY, FASCINATING, AND/OR FUNCTIONAL

Offer children the adventures they've told and you've written down; songs and rhymes they can already recite, in print; read-aloud books; mail, messages, and signs.

 LANGUAGE IS AN INTEGRAL PART OF DAILY LIFE

Continually point out environmental print. Send picture or word messages back and forth. Make read-aloud time as routine as lunch.

 AMPLE OPPORTUNITIES

Encourage "dabbling" with reading and writing with ample opportunities to practice through trial and error, free from criticism, with constructive feedback, and without expecting perfection.

 LANGUAGE IS WHOLE AND COMPLETE

Offer a poem instead of a word list; significant ideas instead of letter drills; natural-sounding sentences instead of stilted, over-simplified ones. The richer print is in meaning to a child, the easier it is to read and the more eager he is to read it. Which three words are more readable: *come, there, up,* or *I love spaghetti?* When written language flows as comfortably as speech, so does reading.

 POSITIVE EXPECTATIONS

Parents assume those first babbles have meaning. Likewise, treat "pretend" reading as "real" reading and first writing attempts as meaningful messages. Children must experience written language as richly and deeply as they experience spoken language, if their reading and writing ability is to be as fluent as their speech.

But learning literacy is not exactly the same process as learning to speak. It does not occur automatically. Indeed, man has not always been a writer nor do all societies possess a written language. Somewhere along the way, people must be shown how to record ideas in print and then read them. Print is a learned code.

THE BLOSSOMING OF READING AND WRITING ABILITY

What are the prerequisites to learning how to read? Children need to clock in thousands of hours of experiencing their world and its spoken and written language, before they can read and write independently. Exploring their world lets them understand the content of what they read. Hearing and using oral language gives them the language structure and vocabulary they need. Experiencing written language lets them understand its meaning, form, and function.

Children can begin this experience from the time they can see and hear. Learning to read does not begin with the first word a child sounds out. Instead it begins when a baby examines a board book or hears his mother sing the words of a song. The *beginning reader* may chime in on a familiar refrain in a read-aloud story or retell a book he's heard read aloud, on his own. Although the *developing reader* may not accurately read the words, he makes the association that print

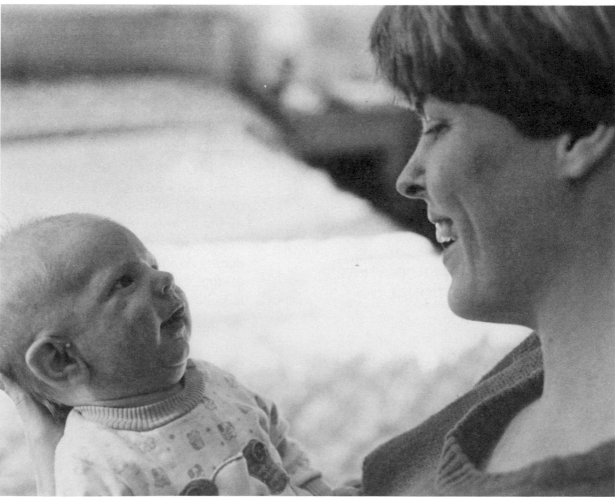

carries meaning. He may read environmental print, favorite words, and follow along on the refrain of a story. The *independent reader* is on his own. He's adept at using a variety of skills to figure out what the print says.

Learning to write does not begin with the first word a child traces. Instead it starts with a *beginning writer's* scribbles and continues with a *developing writer's* "pretend writing" of an important message. The *independent writer* has a working knowledge of the skills it takes to put his ideas into print.

As with speech, ability grows from the random and inaccurate use of language to the refined and sophisticated. Ample opportunities to explore and use written language allow reading and writing ability to blossom. The beauty of allowing children to explore print freely and with your guidance is that they can do so at their own ability level. For example, if you offer pencil and paper to a toddler, he'll likely make scribbles; a child may write about his adventures; and a Shakespeare may create a masterpiece! Each experiences written language at a level matched perfectly to his abilities. Learning is neither forced nor limited.

LEARNING TO READ BY READING; LEARNING TO WRITE BY WRITING

To bring out the born reader in every child, it's our role to offer guidance and a multitude of experiences with written language. In the past, children were offered nonprint "readiness activities" as a way to "get ready for reading." Although shape and sound discrimination and eye-hand coordination activities are valuable and productive, there is no research to show that these activities are prerequisite to learning literacy, nor that they allow children to become better readers and writers. These kinds of activities are offered in this book as a way to increase children's knowledge of the world and to build language skills as they talk about their discoveries. But again, they are not direct literacy-building activities. If we want children to read, the appropriate "readiness" activity is not a puzzle. Instead, we must offer them books and ourselves as reading models. If we want children to write, appropriate preparation is not a bead-stringing exercise. Instead, we must provide pens, paper, print models, and encourage the free exploration of writing.

Children should never be excluded from the literacy activities they so vitally need, simply because they are not yet able readers and writers. At the same time, we should not expect immediate perfection in these skills. As we've discussed, first reading may consist of chiming in on familiar words of a read-aloud story. Accept this as reading because it's truly a discovery of meaning in print. First writing may consist of scribbles. Accept this as writing because it's a real attempt to write a meaningful message.

As with spoken language, it takes years of exploration, experience, and use to master written language. Patience pays off. Children who are given repeated opportunities to freely explore written language at their own pace become, not just capable readers, but enthusiastic ones.

GUIDED LEARNING

Along with ample opportunities to freely explore written language, children need guidance. As children grow from beginning, to developing, to independent readers and writers, your role changes. Here is an overview of the roles you'll assume:

 MODEL

In the beginning, you are a "literacy model." Your child observes you using reading and writing as an integral part of your life. In addition, you model reading by reading aloud to your child. You model writing by acting as your child's scribe, writing down his ideas for him.

 SUPPORTER

As his reading and writing skills develop, you provide support. For the developing reader, you offer strategies for figuring out the code of print to know what written language says. You show the developing writer how to take his ideas and put them into that code.

 CONSULTANT

After your child can read and write independently, you are still there as a consultant. You offer him the right reading material to keep up his enthusiasm for reading. You are the audience and "positive literary critic" for his writing. Because reading and writing are part of a family of communication skills, social interaction is an essential ingredient of the learning process. That interaction takes place with you! Specific activities and details of how to work with your child are given in the following chapters.

THE READING PROCESS

How do readers figure out what the print says? Getting meaning from print involves more than sounding out words. Actually, we use three kinds of knowledge to unlock meaning from print. The first is our knowledge of the world. A reader would have difficulty understanding a passage of text about spiders, if spiders were completely outside his realm of experience.

We also use knowledge of language structure. Word order and grammar affect meaning. *The spider spins a web* makes sense. *Web the spins spider* does not.

And we use knowledge of letter-sound correspondence or phonics.

Fluent readers draw on these three kinds of knowledge simultaneously as they read. For example, let's say *web* is an unknown word in the preceding example. The reader would use his understanding of the topic to realize that a web is what a spider spins; structure to check that *web* is the sort of word that could make sense; and phonics to confirm that the word on the page begins with the /w/ sound of *web*. So an understanding of the world and of the language we speak, along with phonics, are at the very heart of the reading process.

LANGUAGE COMMUNICATION SKILLS

Reading is but one element of language communication. Along with listening, it's a way of receiving information. Writing and speaking are ways of conveying information. These elements are fused by thinking and driven by the desire for meaning. Because they are so interrelated and mutually reinforcing, learning to think, listen, speak, and write must accompany learning to read in a *whole learning process*.

Experience is the starting point. A child is motivated to read a story about a dog, if he's met one, or, even better, walked, fed, and cuddled one. With ample opportunities to talk about the dog's cheerfully wagging tail, and moist, black nose, he'll find meaning in these words when he rediscovers them in print. A desire to share his experience with Grandma may motivate him to write or have you write a letter. By writing, he learns that print is a vital tool for conveying his important ideas.

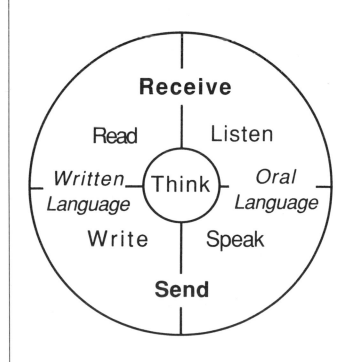

VALUING WRITTEN LANGUAGE

Because children value what serves their interests, reading and writing must do just that: enjoying a pleasurable book instead of filling in a worksheet, or helping Mom write the shopping list instead of memorizing a word list. When this occurs, children read more. And with more reading comes more competence and enjoyment. The cycle continues as children independently strengthen reading skills through their new love of reading. Children are eager to read and write when they discover that written language can communicate ideas *they* find important.

SUMMARY

In brief, the key principles of *Growing Up Reading* are:

1 Learning to read print must support the discovery process that begins at birth, expanding the child's growing knowledge of the world.

2 Children must see reading as the discovery of ideas from print. Skills are essential, but they are learned as tools for this discovery, not as ends in themselves.

3 Because they're so interrelated and mutually reinforcing, learning to think, listen, speak, and write must accompany learning to read.

4 Children must have opportunities to put their own ideas into print to learn the importance of their thoughts, as well as the function and dynamics of written language.

5 Written language must be rich in meaning to children and experienced in whole form as communication vital to the pursuit of *their* unique interests.

These fundamental principles are crucial to your child's becoming a successful reader who loves to read. Take pleasure in sharing the joys of learning and loving to read with your child!

CHAPTER 2

Experience and Comprehension

SENSORY EXPLORATION, CONCEPT BUILDING, CRITICAL THINKING

Discovering meaning is the heart of reading comprehension and the focus of a child's endless quest to understand her world. The richness of her daily experiences combined with the breadth of language she acquires to define these experiences are crucial to her understanding of what she reads. When a child visits a zoo, helps you shop, or hikes in the park, she can bring these experiences to the page to comprehend what she reads. It's easier to understand a story about a farm if you've been there. You can tie *barn, silo,* and *tractor* to your personal experience and bring the story to life. But learning about the world also happens right in your kitchen or backyard. Given opportunities to explore, children will make discoveries and learn language that will not only make them more knowledgeable, but better readers and writers as well.

HOW CHILDREN LEARN

Children learn best from the discoveries they make when they playfully explore and interact with their world. When block towers tumble, children learn about stability and gravity. They begin to understand volume as they pour sand from cup to cup. They learn about properties of liquids through water play. Children construct knowledge by drawing conclusions from their experimentation. Unlike rote learning, their own discoveries stay within them, ready to apply to new situations and their reading. They learn more when they initiate and pursue their own learning, instead of listening to lessons taught by someone else. Creative play is the work of children.

Children engaged in such highly interactive, self-directed exploration are completely absorbed in their work because the process is so fascinating and so much learning is taking place.

Give children language to describe their discoveries. As they mold clay, ask if it's *slimy, slippery, crumbly, smooth.* . . . As they run through autumn leaves, ask if they're *crackly, damp, colorful, deep.* . . . As they taste a pickle, ask if it's *sour, crunchy, crisp, drippy.* . . . They'll know what these words mean when they later encounter them in reading and they'll use those words to enrich their writing.

SENSORY EXPLORATION AND CONCEPT BUILDING

Children receive information through their senses, so sensory development helps children gain knowledge. The opportunities for sensory exploration that you provide help build concepts as well as sharpen perceptions and expand vocabulary.

Materials that encourage open-ended play (not restricted to a single, predetermined use) are the best toys you can offer. The possibilities for making discoveries and discussing them are unlimited with sand, water, and paint. Such materials promote exploration and discovery.

 SAND

Mix, mold, pour, and dig in sand. What's sand like when it's dry, damp, or wet? Explore with:

> **Measuring cups**
> **Molds**
> **Measuring spoons**
> **Shovels**
> **Sieves**
> **Funnels**

ACTIVITIES TO DO AND TO TALK ABOUT:

- Add varying amounts of water to sand. Talk about changes in the sand's consistency.
- Use measuring cups as molds to create "big, bigger, and biggest" sand cakes.
- Make sand sculpture and talk about its creation.
- Sift sand free of stones and twigs.
- Make mountains and dig holes and tunnels.

WATER

Water is readily available and very versatile. It can be enjoyed in the bathtub, a wading pool, or even a small basin. Remember that *water play always requires adult supervision.* Equip your young explorer with tools for discovery.

> **Plastic bottles**
> **Sponges**
> **Plastic tubing**
> **Funnels**
> **Meat basters**
> **Measuring cups**
> **Spray bottles**
> **Medicine droppers**

ACTIVITIES TO DO AND TO TALK ABOUT:

- Wash dolls, clothing, rocks, dishes.
- Beat soapy water with an egg beater. What happens?
- Blow soap bubbles with wands and trumpets. How are bubbles alike and different?
- Observe and talk about how food coloring mixes with water.
- Experiment with placing corks, feathers, coins, or rocks in the water. Which items sink and which float?
- "Paint" things outdoors with a large brush and water.
- Freeze and boil water while your child observes. Talk about what's happening.
- Punch various hole patterns in the bottoms of plastic bottles. Describe how the water flows out.

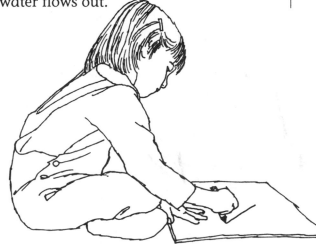

 PAINT

Children love to paint — if they're allowed to paint whatever they want and according to their own rules. Brushing bright colors on paper is fun, but also try painting with:

> **Cotton swabs**
> **Sponges**
> **Sticks**
> **Corks**
> **Feathers**
> **Marbles**
> **Fingers**
> **Toes**
> **String**

ACTIVITIES TO DO AND TO TALK ABOUT:

- Drip paint on paper and fold it in half.
- Use water color on wet paper.
- Fingerpaint.
- Dip string in paint, then drag on paper.
- Dip a marble in paint, then roll it on paper set in a tray.
- Place a dab of thin paint on paper, then move it around by blowing through a straw.
- Dip various objects in a tray of paint. Use them to "print" shapes on the paper.
- Cut up dry paintings and paste them together to create a new picture.

Opportunities for concept-building through sensory exploration can be found in other materials such as clay, blocks, and construction toys. Cooking opens the world of taste and smell. Explore the world of sound by making and listening to sounds and music. The possibilities are almost endless. Have fun coming up with more.

Remember, to prepare your child for reading and writing, talk together about her exploration. Share a wealth of language to define the properties ("This stone feels *hard* and *smooth*"), relationships ("Your block is *heavier* than mine"), and concepts she discovers ("It's easier to ride my bike downhill than uphill").

DEVELOPING CRITICAL THINKING SKILLS

Children have an enormous data collection capacity. To organize and use information they collect, they need to think critically. It's also true for reading. They'll use critical thinking skills to organize the information gained from reading for problem-solving in life. Let's look at ways to develop critical thinking skills.

 CLASSIFYING

Your young child recognizes the sameness of all four-legged, barking tail-waggers and labels them *dogs*. She identifies all those hard, round things on the ground as *rocks* and not as *dogs*. Soon she can distinguish a particular kind of dog or rock. She uses critical thinking skills to classify dogs sharing a common characteristic into sub-categories such as poodle, setter, or terrier.

Your child already classifies as she decides which belongings go into the toy chest, clothing drawer, or bookcase. Help her develop classification skills through games such as this one. Think of a category, such as *animals*. Take turns naming as many as you can. Now focus on specific characteristics and think of animals that fit into each of these sub-categories: *animals that fly, animals living in water, furry animals, four-legged animals*, and so on. You can even take *animals that fly* and further categorize them into *birds* and *insects*.

Help your child apply this skill to reading by talking about classification when you read a book aloud together. For example, after reading Eric Carle's *The Very Hungry Caterpillar*, she can group the foods the caterpillar ate into those she would enjoy eating and those she wouldn't. Then have her think carefully about those foods. Which grew on trees? Which needed to be cooked? Which were sweet?

 SEQUENCING

Sequencing is putting events in order: "*First*, we went to the market. *Then*, we bought the groceries. *Next*, we unpacked the food at home." With this thinking skill, your child determines what comes first, next, and last to comprehend a story or instructions: "The *first* pig used straw to build his home. The *second* pig used sticks, and the *third* used bricks." Build an awareness of sequencing by talking together and identifying the order of events of a special experience or a favorite story.

We also sequence to read and write from left to right. Sequence is closely related to prediction, a crucial skill for reading comprehension. When we make a prediction, we anticipate a sequence of events.

 PREDICTING

Your child sees the morning sun shine, remembers how hot it was yesterday, and predicts that shorts will be ideal attire. She smells a familiar aroma in the kitchen and looks forward to soup for lunch.

Reading revolves around making predictions: We anticipate what a book will be about from its cover; we predict the meaning of unknown words from the other known words in the sentence; we speculate what will happen next as we read, modify our prediction based on new information we receive, then read on to discover the outcome. Prediction propels us forward through the print. Improving your child's prediction skills enhances her ability to understand what she reads and helps her maintain interest in the story.

Talk about what predictions are. Model how to make a prediction as you read a story aloud. Invite your child to make predictions by asking, "What do you think will happen next?" Then comment, "That's interesting. Let's read more and see." Questions such as these develop this powerful comprehension tool:

- What surprise do you think Grandpa is bringing you?
- What do you think Halloween will be like this year?
- Can you finish this rhyme: *Jack and Jill went up the . . .?*
- Predict how *Middle-Sized Billy Goat Gruff* will get across the bridge?
- Do you think *Harry, the Dirty Dog* will ever go back home?
- Will the *Magic Fish* continue to grant the old man's wishes?

Always add, "What makes you think so?" Help your child amend her predictions as she gathers more information. For example, "You thought the Little Red Hen would bake bread for all the farmyard animals. Now that you see they won't even help her plant the wheat, do you want to stick with your prediction or make a new one?" Have fun reading on to discover the outcome.

BUILDING THINKING SKILLS

Problem solving occurs at different levels of complexity. Solving the problem of how many glasses are needed on the table is easier than solving the problem of what meal to serve five people with differing tastes. And that's easier to solve than the problem of world hunger. The types of questions you ask can build your child's thinking skills for effective problem solving. Applying these questions to reading material builds thinking skills while helping children get the most learning and enjoyment from their reading.

Let's look at three types of skill-building questions: *knowledge, understanding,* and *creative thinking* questions. *Knowledge* questions help children recall basic information from the story. For example, after reading *Three Billy Goats Gruff* you might ask, "What sizes were the Billy Goats?" Although answering this question involves no more than remembering facts, the increasing sizes of the goats is critical to understanding the plot. An *understanding* question helps children comprehend why events are happening. "Why did the troll let Little Billy Goat Gruff cross the bridge?" *Creative thinking* questions invite children to use information imaginatively, beyond recall and understanding of facts. "How might you and your sister cross a bridge with a troll in charge?" "Do you think it was right for Big Billy Goat Gruff to knock the troll into the water? Why or why not?"

Thinking skills can be built through the informal conversations you share about familiar stories (for example, *Goldilocks and the Three Bears*), television shows (*Sesame Street*), and life experiences (Thanksgiving dinner). Ask questions in the spirit of exploration, not testing. Never ask so many questions that you interfere with your child's enjoyment of a story or event. The following are sample questions:

 ## KNOWLEDGE

Knowledge questions help the child recall basic elements of the story or event.

- How many bears were in the story?
- Who did you see on *Sesame Street* today?
- Can you remember what we ate at Thanksgiving dinner?

 ## UNDERSTANDING

Understanding information is knowing how and why.

- Why did the bears go for a walk?
- What problem did Bert and Ernie face?
- Draw one picture of how the table looked before we ate Thanksgiving dinner, one picture while we were eating, and another after we ate.

 ## CREATIVE THINKING

Having information is important, but children need opportunities to apply that information in imaginative ways and to their own lives. Creative-thinking questions stimulate children to solve problems, make judgments, categorize information, and come up with totally new ideas.

- Draw a picture of how you think *Goldilocks and the Three Bears* should end.
- Have you ever faced a situation similar to what Goldilocks faced? What did you do?
- Let's make up our own story, *Taylor and the Three Aliens.*
- How are you and Ernie alike? Different?
- What would you have done if you were Big Bird?
- Let's invent our own holiday. How will we celebrate it?

Once upon a time there were 3 aliens.

SENSORY EXPLORATION AND CONCEPT BUILDING

SENSORY MATCHING AND ORDERING

Help your child discover physical characteristics through her senses and share this knowledge through language.

 DARK AND LIGHT

Cut out different color blocks from free paint-sample cards to make two identical color sets. Let her match colors from one set with those from the other. Now, cut out color blocks of shades of a single color. Can she arrange pinks, greens, or blues from lightest shade to darkest? Talk about the intensity of the colors.

 ROUGH AND SMOOTH

Cut two 3" x 3" squares from each of several different grades of sandpaper and one sheet of smooth cardboard. Make two identical sets of each of these different squares. Let her first match textures from one set with its pair in the other; then sequence one set of papers from smoothest to roughest. Can she do this blindfolded, relying only on her sense of touch? Talk about the variety of textures she feels.

LOUD AND QUIET

Fill pairs of 35 mm film canisters or similar small containers with: beans, rice, sand, seeds, coins, paper clips, bolts, or pebbles. Leave one pair empty. Seal the lids using contrasting colors of tape to identify each set. Let your child first match each can from one set with its mate in the other by shaking and listening to the sound; then order the cans from quietest to loudest. Talk about the intensity and variety of sounds.

 TASTES

Make two identical sets of paper cups filled with food samples to taste and match: salty (salt), sweet (sugar), sour (lemon), spicy (spices), and bitter (instant coffee). Talk about the variety of flavors.

 ODORS

Fill each pair of small containers with: spices, onion slices, and cotton balls soaked in perfume, vanilla, peppermint, or other flavoring extracts. Use contrasting stickers or tape to identify each set. Let your child smell a container from one set, then match its odor with a container from the other set. Talk about the variety of scents.

VISUAL AWARENESS

Talk about the visual differences and similarities your child discovers through these activities.

 WHAT DO YOU SEE?

Invite your child to describe an object or scene she sees while on a drive or walk. Ask questions to help her see details. "You see a river. What do you see on the banks of the river?"

 PUZZLES

Your child learns about visual relationships by linking parts of the picture to create the whole. Try making your own puzzles. Paste a magazine picture onto a sturdy piece of cardboard. Cut into pieces according to her ability. Let her put it back together. It's fun to use photos of your child or family. She can make her own picture on stiff paper, cut it apart, and try to reassemble it.

 PHOTO RECALL

Next time you process film, have two copies made of each photo. Your child will now have a personalized set of cards to play *Match, Recall,* and *Pairs* (see *Activities,* chapter 5).

 OBJECT-SHAPE MATCH

Trace around several objects on a piece of cardboard to outline their shapes. Set them off the board and let your child put each object back in place.

AUDITORY AWARENESS

Together, spend a few minutes, in silence with your eyes closed, identifying sounds in your home or neighborhood. Collect sounds by tape-recording them, if you can. What makes each sound: people, animals, machinery? Describe them: soft, low-pitched, screechy, sharp.

TASTE & ODOR AWARENESS

Talk about the smells and tastes of a meal you are enjoying. For fun, let her eat a meal blindfolded. Can she tell what she's eating by its smell and taste? Help her describe her meal. Now it's your turn to try!

TACTILE AWARENESS

Let your child describe what she's touching. As she pets a dog or plays in the sand pile, encourage her to talk about the way things feel. She can also try the following activities. To really focus in on tactile awareness, she can try them blindfolded.

 BOTTLE TOPS

Match a variety of bottles and jars with their proper lids.

 NUTS AND BOLTS

Match a collection of nuts and bolts. Then put them in order from smallest to largest.

 MYSTERY OBJECT

Put familiar objects (brush, spoon, or small toys) into a bag. Let your child identify and describe each one by feel, then check herself by pulling it out. You can also ask her to find a particular object: "Can you feel the spoon?"

CLASSIFYING

SORTING EVERYDAY EXPERIENCES

What may seem like a chore to you can be exciting, thinking-skill practice for your child. Remember to talk about the characteristics you are using for sorting criteria.

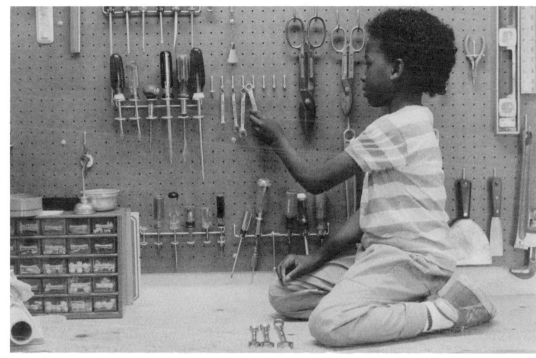

 SHOPPING

Point out how markets and shops classify merchandise. Let your child help locate the apples, ice cream, or milk. Back home, unpack your groceries together according to your system of storage. You can also give her an assortment of food or empty containers to sort into piles: grain, vegetable, canned, bottled, boxed.

 KITCHEN UTENSILS

Let your child put silverware away by sorting knives, spoons, and forks. Sort plastic dishes by size or use.

 LAUNDRY

Match socks or sort clothing by owner, color, fabric, or type.

 TOYS

Sort toys into groups of vehicles, dolls, books, infant toys, or child's toys.

 HARDWARE

Garages are full of neat things to sort: bolts, nuts, nails by size; tools by use; sandpaper by texture or grade.

 GOING TO THE LIBRARY

Talk about how the library sorts books. Children's materials are grouped together in one location. Within that location, they are further sorted into picture books, fiction, nonfiction, records, and tapes. Now let your child find her library materials.

PEOPLE SORT

Collect photographs of people from newspapers, magazines, and family photos. Print category titles clearly on index cards. Lay them out with a sample picture beneath each one. Let your child make columns of pictures under each heading. By focusing on certain characteristics, she'll discover that people grouped in one category can also be in different categories, too.

Feelings: happy, sad, angry, frightened

Ages: babies, children, teens, adults, seniors

Sexes: male, female

Activities: at work, at play,

OBJECT SORT

Set out some small objects along with index cards labeled *yes* and *no* (or use happy and sad faces for pre-readers). Pose a question such as, "Does it float?" Let your child decide by placing each object in a bowl of water, then setting it beneath the correct response. Use a magnet to test the objects and answer the question, "Is it magnetic?" She can answer "What is it made of?" by sorting the objects beneath word cards and sample objects: *plastic, cloth,* or *wood.* A variation of this activity would be to give your child several shoe boxes with these same labels. Then, send her off to find a boxful of small objects made from each material.

MUFFIN TIN SORT

Mix up handfuls of items like macaroni, buttons, pebbles, paper clips, bobby pins, and pennies in a bowl. Place and name a sample object in each section of a muffin tin or egg carton. Let your child sort the rest into the correct sections of the tin.

CATEGORY COLLAGE

Have your child find pictures in magazines pertaining to a particular category. She can make a collage by cutting them out and pasting them on a sheet of paper. For example, she can make separate collages of people, animals, furniture, food, or any other easy-to-find magazine photos. Keep these sheets in a binder to make a category scrapbook.

COLLECTIONS

Maintaining a good, old-fashioned collection helps children categorize. Items such as stamps, coins, leaves, seeds, rocks, shells, dried plants, and beads lend themselves to collecting and categorizing. Talk about the similarities and differences among the objects within a collection. Try to classify the objects into sub-categories such as igneous rocks or French coins.

ENVIRONMENTS

Match each element to its environment by placing small cards beneath the sky, land, or water card. (See page 141 for activity materials.)

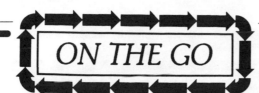

ON THE GO

 BRAINSTORM

Brainstorm and list things that belong in a particular category such as:

- Living things
- Things in a pet store
- Things that crawl
- Things babies do
- Noisy things.

 CLASSIFY IT

Think of two or three colors, textures, or other characteristics. Take turns naming items, letting the other person classify them. "Our categories are red, yellow, and blue. In which category would a banana be? Which for your overalls?" A rose might fit into more than one color category. Explain the reasons for your choices.

 ALIKE AND DIFFERENT

Compare and contrast ways things are alike and different. Pets, people, places, objects are all fair game. How is Michael's dog like/different from Allison's? How is Grandma's house like/different from ours?

 SPOT IT!

Talk about the different ways to categorize things your child can see on an outing. In the fall for example, discuss the characteristics of deciduous and evergreen trees. Then on an outing, have your child call out, "deciduous", or "evergreen" when she spots these kinds of trees. Other things to distinguish among include:

- Vans, sedans, station wagons
- Cyclists, motorists, equestrians, pedestrians
- Solids, liquids, gases
- Opaque, transparent, translucent

You'll be introducing new vocabulary as well as categorization skill.

 ODD MAN OUT

List several objects and let your child decide which one doesn't belong. Have her explain why. For example, "raincoat, umbrella, bathing suit, boots" or "milk, juice, car, pizza." You can even introduce the concept of subcategorizing by then asking, "milk, juice, pizza, soda" (pizza is not a *liquid* food). Now let her set the game up for you to try.

 WHAT'S THE CATEGORY?

Older children will enjoy this challenging game. Start it out by saying, "I'm going on a trip, and I'm taking a pencil, a straw, and telephone pole." Now without identifying the category, let each child take turns repeating the list and adding an object that fits into the same group. "I'm going on a trip, and I'm taking a pencil, a straw, a telephone pole, and a stick." Let all players decide whether or not the added object fits into the same category as the others.

 LITERARY SORT

Build literary awareness by discussing stories you've read together. Which are adventures, folk tales, or nature stories? In which do sad characters become happy, poor become rich, or the lonely find friends? In which are characters granted three wishes or must accomplish three tasks? Which start with "Once upon a time"?

Familiar characters can be sorted into categories: animal heroes, human heroes, villains, friendly monsters, wise or foolish characters. Now compare and contrast them. How are Goldilocks and Red Riding Hood alike? Whose life was more difficult, Cinderella's or Snow White's? Remember, there are no right or wrong answers. These questions serve as springboards to stimulate thinking and literary awareness.

SEQUENCING AND PREDICTION

COMIC MIX–UP

Paste a comic strip onto stiff paper. Cut apart the squares. Let your child arrange them in proper order by anticipating what comes next.

BEANS, BUTTONS, PENNIES

Repeat a pattern of objects two and a half times. Then, let your child predict which objects come next and complete and repeat the pattern. For example:
Bean-bean-bean-penny-penny-bean-bean-bean-penny-penny-bean. . . .
                    or
Button-button-bean-penny-bean-button-button-bean-penny-bean-button. . .
Patterns can increase in complexity.

PICTURE MY DAY OR STORY

Write sentences describing a day's events on separate sheets of paper. Read the sentences to your child for her to illustrate. Shuffle the illustrated sheets. Then let her lay them out in order, moving from left to right, describing each one. You can also picture a future occurrence and predict its sequence of events. "First we'll clean the house. Then we'll bake a cake. Next my friends will arrive for my birthday!" Also try picturing events from a favorite tale.

PREDICTION CARDS

Have your child put each set in order, laying cards out from left to right, telling the story and predicting the outcome. (See page 142 for activity materials.)

ON THE GO

 PLANNING MY DAY

Sequence previous or future events. For example, your child can plan and predict what she'll do today. "First I woke up. Next I'll get dressed. Then . . ."

 AS TIME GOES BY

Discuss the effect of time on: your growing child, a plant developing from seed, the landscape changing with the seasons. You can also use the family photo album to discuss and predict changes in your child and others. "How do you think your baby cousin will look when we see her next?" For fun, she can put photos of herself at different ages in chronological order.

 RETELL THE STORY

Let your child tell you a familiar story, putting the events in order. She can retell a story you've just read aloud or use a picture book to help guide her in discovering the story's sequence. "First, the girl tries to fly by running and jumping. Then, she makes herself paper wings. Next, the postman delivers a magic egg . . ." (from Shirley Hughes's *Up and Up*).

 HOW-TO-DO-IT

Talk about carpentry, gardening, or other activities performed in a set order. "I'm baking cookies. First, I assemble my ingredients. What do you think I'll do next?" Show how you refer to the recipe for the sequence. You can share a craft project referring back to the instruction manual. She can tell you the steps of an activity such as how to play a game.

CHAPTER 3

Language

COMMUNICATING IDEAS
THROUGH SPEECH

Babbling, singing, roaring, listening, and just plain talking are all forms of language communication children explore. Children love language. They talk to you, their friends, pets, toys, themselves — anyone who will listen, and even those who won't. Children don't learn to speak through lessons. They learn language by being totally immersed in it and by having ample opportunities to put it to use.

WHY ENCOURAGE ORAL LANGUAGE DEVELOPMENT?

Spoken language, like written language, is vital communication. We listen and read to understand, and we speak and write to be understood. Printed language derives from oral language, so children need a rich oral vocabulary and knowledge of language structure to comprehend ideas communicated in print. Oral and written language ability build on each other.

LISTENING AND TALKING

It's amazing how rapidly children acquire language, with all its complexity, within the first years of life. Most know about 2,000 words by their fifth birthday. Their use and comprehension of language are remarkably sophisticated by that time. Children learn language best through social interaction with a caring adult. They model the language you offer. Language ability thrives when a child experiences its power in affecting his world: babbled first words bring Mom's delighted response; later, saying "milk" results in quenched thirst.

Here's how to encourage language to flow during these unique first years of life. Examples are given for enriching language during daily interaction as well as in reaction to a read-aloud book.

MODEL LANGUAGE

Even your baby needs you as a language model. Although a response may be some time away, he's taking in language now for an incredible language explosion to come. When he's playing near you, describe in detail everything you're doing. "I'm washing the dishes. The water is warm and bubbly. Now I'm washing a cup. It's smooth and hard. . . ." Most everyday tasks interest him: gardening, driving, or shopping. Also describe what your baby is doing. Ask questions, then give him time to respond with sounds. Doing so instills a self-concept that he is indeed a "speaker" by acknowledging his participation in this vital form of communication. "Kevin is climbing on the sofa. It must feel soft. Where is Kevin climbing now?"

After reading a book aloud to your child, such as *The Snowy Day* by Ezra Jack Keats, you can model language by sharing your reactions: "That story reminds me of when I was a little girl and my friend Ann and I lay down in the snow and made angels with our bodies."

 BUILD AWARENESS

"How does that carrot taste? Sweet or sour? Is it soft or crunchy?" Or ask, "How would it feel to touch the snow in the morning?" (reacting to *The Snowy Day*).

 EXTEND CONVERSATION

Build on your child's words and experiences. You can increase his vocabulary by embellishing his sentences. If your child says, "There's a dog," you might reply, "Yes, there is a brown, furry dog. It looks like Aunt Sarah's Wolfy, except this dog has shorter legs. What else is different about this dog?" Or say, "Yes, you can build a snowman in the snow. What else could you build?" (reacting to *The Snowy Day*).

Extending conversation is also a way to give your child constructive feedback as he experiments with grammar. If he says, "I drawed a picture." You can respond, "Yes, you *drew* a very colorful picture." You provide a correct model, without being critical, by simply restating words.

 PROMOTE THINKING

Open-ended questions encourage thinking about new possibilities. "What would make your friend happy?" Or after reading *The Snowy Day*, "Remember when it snowed in our town? What special things could you do in the backyard that you couldn't do any other day?"

 SPARK IMAGINATION

Stretch imagination and arouse natural curiosity. "Which animal at the pet store would you like to be? What would your life be like if a child chose you as his pet?" Again reacting to *The Snowy Day*, "What would happen if ice cream snowed from the sky?"

The first pig built a house of straw.

The second pig built a house of sticks.

The third pig built a house of bricks.

CHANTS, SONGS, AND RHYMES

Classic nursery rhymes, chants, and songs provide the perfect bridge between speaking and reading. When the familiar words children say become the same words they read, reading success is guaranteed.

There's wisdom in sharing the classic rhymes that are so much a part of our cultural and literary heritage with our children. These rhymes celebrate language, transferring its rhythm, flow, and structure to our budding speakers, readers, and writers.

Language is composed of a multitude of patterns. With their intrinsic desire to master language, children "study" these patterns on their own, as they chant rhymes in their play and repeatedly ask to hear them. In the process, they assimilate the patterns and structure of language they'll need for reading and writing fluency. This familiarity with language develops an expectation for what the words will say when children encounter the rhyme in print.

Just as we bring our life experiences to the page to discover meaning, we also bring along our knowledge of language structure. Rhymes are filled with language structure. When children learn rhymes, they can apply this knowledge of language structure to their reading and writing. So, enjoy singing and reciting together. Also, offer audio recordings of classic and new children's songs.

READING WHOLE LANGUAGE

Typically, beginning readers memorize words in isolation and learn to sound out words before they read sentences and stories. But recognizing or sounding out the word *shoe* can be a far more difficult task than reading this entire, flowing sentence, *1,2, Buckle my shoe.*

Also, the language of reading primers is often contrived to make it "easier" to read. Although *Pip can tip a lid* may be consistent with rules of phonics, it's inconsistent with what children know of language. This over-simplification makes such a sentence a chore to read and children fail to perceive reading as the discovery of meaning.

In contrast, the rhymes your child has mastered make ideal first reading material. Their familiarity lets him anticipate the words and discover meaning. So to assure an instantly successful first reading experience, we'll start your child reading written language in the whole form of a familiar rhyme.

LET'S READ 1, 2!

This activity is perfect for children who love to learn and chant rhymes. If this description doesn't fit your child, wait. In the meantime, expose him to rhymes by chanting them to him and playing recordings of children's songs and rhymes. Soon he'll be chiming in and eventually chanting the entire rhyme on his own.

Those who enjoy chanting rhymes can be introduced to their favorites in print. Familiarize your child with the rhyme, *1, 2, Buckle My Shoe* by chanting it together informally over a period of time. When he can recite it independently with ease, present him with the *First Reading Book* entitled, *1, 2!* (see page 143 for activity materials). Because he has already previewed the rhyme, he'll be able to predict what the printed words will say. This first reading experience will be one of roughly matching the printed words with the ones in his memory.

Chant and read *1,2!* as you follow along with your finger beneath the words. Then chant, leaving out the word at the end of the phrase. Pause to let him predict and read the word you point to. "1,2, Buckle my . . . " Now let him chant by himself as you again point to the words. Don't expect him to read word for word. At this point he is making the general association between the words he can say and those in print.

After mastering the 1,2! rhyme, he can create his own version: "1,2, A kangaroo. 3,4, An angry boar."

You can transform any favorite rhyme, or new child-composed version, into a song-book. Songs with a refrain such as *Old MacDonald* or *The Farmer in the Dell* are ideal because their structures are so clear. Children easily retain and retrieve the words from their memory. See chapter 7, *Creating Books*, for instructions. Or, use a rhyme book from chapter 9, the *Treasury*.

By reading familiar songs, your child sees the same word pattern that he can already say represented in print. He realizes that written language comprises separate words that are spoken and written in the same sequence. And reading isn't merely sounding out words and stringing them together. It's uncovering real meaning about a buckled shoe, a twinkling star, or a noisy farm.

By creating his own versions, he experiences the dynamics and power of language.

LISTENING AND TALKING

 SENTENCE TALK

Say a sentence. Talk about how it is made up of individual words. Now write it out. Point to each word as you say it again. Read a sentence in a book while you point to each word. Show your child how our spoken words can be recorded in print.

 JUST LISTEN

Play recordings of children's stories and songs while your child plays. Portable tape players (set at low volume!) along with favorite tape cassettes can develop listening skills during boring meetings or long car trips.

WORDSTORMING

Enrich your child's vocabulary and knowledge of language structure, both for speaking now and writing in the future. Stretch imagination and vocabulary fully by brainstorming together as many words as you can to describe whatever interests him. For example, foods, vehicles, or snakes make good subjects. Your child will have much to say about a subject from a nonfiction book you've just shared. Wordstorm to generate words, sentences, and books.

 WORDS

For example, let's use snakes. Wordstorm for adjectives that describe snakes. After you have many words, wordstorm verbs to tell how snakes move. Then wordstorm for prepositional phrases that tell where snakes go.
Snakes: long, skinny, scaly. . .
How snakes move: wiggle, slither, wind, glide . . .
Where a snake might go: under a rock, to the pond, through tall grass . . .

 SENTENCES

Once you've generated many words and phrases, write the words or phrases on the backs of business cards. Manipulate the cards to create a variety of sentences: *Sea snakes swim under water; Long snakes glide through tall grass; Grass snakes lay eggs under logs.*

 BOOKS

Make a snake book by writing each sentence on a page for your child to illustrate.

FOLLOWING DIRECTIONS

This listening skill requires special attention to details. Take turns giving and following each other's instructions.

 STEP BY STEP

Let your child follow one-, two-, or three-step directions. "Put your hands on your hips, close your eyes, now hop." Add the "Simon Says" command for more fun.

 LISTENING PICTURE

Let him draw by listening to instructions. "Draw four red circles across the top of the paper. Color one blue. Draw an X beneath another circle."

 LISTENING SNACK

Let him make a snack by listening to instructions. "Place the celery stick on a plate. Spread peanut butter into the hollow part of the celery. Sprinkle raisins on top. Now eat!"

"Long snakes glide silently through tall grass."

IMAGINATIVE PLAY

There are so many new things to think and talk about when you pretend to be a firefighter, a queen, or one of the Three Bears. Play can be unstructured, or your child might enjoy acting out a story you've read to him. Encourage imaginative play with puppets, old clothes, props, and a special area for a stage.

REAL WORLD READING

Inspire an interest in print along with imaginative play by creating "prop kits." Fill boxes with necessary props for different real world settings. Include print props. For example, the doctor's kit contains the typical toy stethoscope and bandages. But also provide a clipboard, paper, pencil, and prescription forms to encourage your young doctor to read and write. Just add an order pad, pencil, and menu to the cook set and your waiter will be reading and writing as he serves. (See *Dramatic Play*, page 136, for more ideas.) Print is a major part of the real world work settings your child loves to imitate. Make sure it's also part of the make-believe world your child creates.

Make many copies of the forms we've provided. Be on the lookout for castoffs from such sources as stores, offices, restaurants, and mail. (See page 149 for activity materials.)

READING WHOLE LANGUAGE

OLD MACDONALD

This classic song appeals to children because of its refrain, simple structure, and animal sounds. (See page 154 for activity materials.)
1. Place word cards for one verse on the appropriate lines as you both sing the song. Can your child do this by himself? Repeat this step for each verse.
2. Now, mix cards together from two verses. Can he differentiate *baa* from *r-r-r*? Do this together if it's too difficult. Try again after he's learned these letter sounds in chapter 6. But for now, let him simply experience print he can already chant.

Create new songs using the same structure. Make word cards for new verses. Try singing these variations together:

- Your child could own the business: "Gregory Fisher had a ship . . ."
- Old MacDonald might have a lion, a dinosaur, a Zlidge, or a robot, each making strange and unique sounds: "with a bleep, bleep here . . ."
- Perhaps he had a store, a bus, a city, an ocean: "And in this ocean he had some fish . . . with a gurgle, gurgle here . . ."
- Or it's a holiday: "And on this farm he had a ghost . . . with a b-o-o-o here . . ."

Now make an original songbook for your favorite language creation (see chapter 7, *Creating Books*). If it's time for a new song, you can find one in a book of nursery rhymes, children's poetry, or familiar songs (see chapter 9, *Treasury*).

Explore the endless possibilities for manipulating and creating language. Your child will experience the joy, flexibility, and purpose of language and begin to understand the connection between speech and print.

TWINKLE, TWINKLE, LITTLE STAR

The following activities serve as models for using any rhyme as a way to introduce reading skills. Your child will need some knowledge of print and your guidance. Model these activities for an interested beginning reader by pointing to the words as you read them aloud. Do the activity, while he observes.

- Share the *Twinkle* song sheet just as you shared *1,2!*
- Which word is *twinkle?* Find rhyming words, repeating words and sentences.
- Cut apart the sentence strips. Have your child match them to those on the song sheet.
- Shuffle them and let him order them as he sings.
- Use scraps of paper to cover up the ending word of each sentence. Can your child predict the word?
- Create a star songbook by printing the words on star-shaped pages.
- Now try composing an original version: "Babble, babble, little brook." (See page 153 for activity materials.)

ON THE GO

 SHARE A STORY

Take turns telling parts of a story. "One morning when I woke up . . ." Your child continues, "I saw an enormous red elephant staring at me. It said . . ." You continue, "I'm starving . . ."

 SING A SONG

Turn a boring trip into a musical fest. Introduce your child to any favorite song. Invite him to join in. Camp songs are great fun with their repeating refrains and opportunities to create silly versions.

 CLUES

Let your child guess what you're thinking of from the clues you give him. Use new vocabulary as you describe the unknown. "I'm thinking of a ferocious animal. It's larger than your bed . . ." Literary characters and books are fun to guess. "I'm thinking of a little boy who was sent to bed without any dinner . . ." (Max from *Where the Wild Things Are*). Now, let him think of something and give you clues. A variation is to let your child solicit clues by asking you yes/no questions about the mystery item. "Is it a food? Is it round?"

 HERE'S WHAT'S HERE

Take turns naming 10 or 20 objects in the living room, garage, or park. Stretch your minds and vocabularies to include such details as pine needles, bark, or pebbles in a park. Think of objects mentioned in a favorite book such as a comb, brush, or bowl of mush from Margaret Wise Brown's *Goodnight, Moon*.

 JOKES AND RIDDLES

The humor of most jokes relies on word play and double meanings. They therefore provide a valuable and playful way to build vocabulary in older children. "What food is yellow and has appeal? A banana." But, younger children can enjoy simple riddles, such as, "I'm thinking of a food. It is long and thin. It has a yellow peel. What is it?" Take turns asking and answering jokes and/or riddles.

 TAKE IT TO MARS

Start by saying, "I'm going to Mars and I'm taking a pizza." Your child says, "I'm going to Mars and I'm taking a pizza and a yo-yo." Each player adds an item, after repeating all others named in order so far. The game can be made more challenging by requiring that items be of the same category such as animals, toys, household items, things in a forest or ocean.

 COMPLETE THE SENTENCE

Encourage language and imagination by inviting your child to complete such humorous or thought-provoking sentences as: "If I had three wishes, I'd . . ." or "If the ocean were filled with lemonade . . ." See *If's* and *Sentence springboards*, pages 98 and 99 for more ideas.

CHAPTER 4

Valuing Reading

I LOVE TO READ!

WHY READ?

Children value reading when they understand why people read. A child hears a story read aloud and understands that reading can bring an exciting adventure to life. She sees you write the grocery list, read product labels, and follow the directions in the recipe book, and she understands that reading is a crucial ingredient in making those yummy chocolate chip cookies. Reading has value because it's both enjoyable and functional.

A child learns the value of reading best through experience. Telling your child that reading is important and enjoyable just won't do the trick. But these actions will:

- Modeling the use of written language
- Helping her read to function in life
- Reading aloud to her
- Providing a print-rich home.

YOU AS MODEL

Children are great imitators. They play "store," "doctor," and "restaurant," attempting to copy the adult world. When you are sweeping the floor, your child is probably the first one to jump in with her little broom. If you're hammering in the garage, you'd better have some extra nails handy.

And so it is with written language. If you rely on print for your daily accomplishments and leisure, so will your child. Let her observe you reading for function: from a menu, a road map, a television program guide, the newspaper. Let her see you reading for pleasure: from an absorbing novel, a cartoon, a magazine, a catalog. Let her also see you write: a shopping list, an appointment schedule, a note to Dad, letters to friends. Encourage your child to join you in these activities. The message will be clear: print contains essential keys for participating in an exciting world.

> We ned
> jam
> milk
> juz
> potatos
> bred
> met
> orngis
> apls
> bunaus
> peanut butr
> cuces

We need jam, milk, juice, potatoes, bread, meat, oranges, apples, bananas, peanut butter, cookies.

FUNCTIONAL READING IN THE REAL WORLD

Printed signs and messages make excellent first-reading material. They are virtually everywhere. They are usually written in large, clear letters. They introduce children to upper-case letters and a variety of type styles. But most importantly, they carry vital information for surviving in the real world.

Reading environmental print lets children experience the genuine need for written communication. Help your child combine phonics skills with critical-thinking skills to figure out what signs say. Talk about the context in which the print appears. What clues near the *Wet Paint* sign alert you to what it says? These context clues along with knowledge of initial letter sounds often provide enough information to understand the sign. "Look at that shiny door. It looks as if it was just painted. I wonder what this sign says? W-W-W-et P-P-P-aint."

Build an awareness that the print around us contains information important to your child, by letting her read, then act on that information. If she needs a restroom, focus her attention on the door signs and let her decide which restroom to use. Follow along with your finger under the word as you sound it out together: "M-M-MEN." Before entering a shop, let her decide if it's open or closed based on the sign on the door. While in the car, let her call out road signs and freeway exits. Tell your child which department store you're looking for in the mall and see if she can recognize its sign.

Point out the names of groceries as you make selections in the market. Help her identify words such as *milk, apple juice,* and the brand name of her breakfast cereal as you shop or set the table at home. Share the words on a snack's package with your child before removing it. Children need to solidly understand the reasons for written language in order to gain control over it and put it to use.

WHY READ ALOUD?

Reading aloud is perhaps the most effective learn-to-read and love-to-read activity you can share with your child. By reading aloud, you become a "book-advocate," enticing your child into an exciting new world of learning and entertainment. You not only instill an appreciation for the fascinating wealth of human experience accessible through print, but you impart a sense of the reading process. Reading aloud lets you explore together meaning in print, making reading a friendly and secure experience.

A child's listening comprehension far exceeds her reading abilities, so reading aloud lets your child "listen up." You can share the joy of books long before your child can read on her own. And it is just as important to continue reading aloud long after she becomes proficient, always stretching comprehension and enjoying a wonderful shared experience.

HOW TO BEGIN

Grab a great book. Cuddle up with your child. And read! You can hardly go wrong. What follows are suggestions for making the very most of this special experience. Your child's age and interests will influence book selection.

 BABIES

Babies love to hear the rhythm of their parent's voice. So read aloud all sorts of material in a very dramatic voice. You can offer plenty of rhythm and rhyme with nursery rhymes. Even while changing diapers recite those same nursery rhymes from books you enjoyed together. Read to your baby while she is feeding to make reading aloud a nurturing experience. If your baby is near while you're reading your own book or newspaper, go ahead and read portions aloud. Share books that show familiar scenes and objects from your baby's world. Even if your baby is too young to respond, invite her participation by asking and then pointing out where familiar items are on the page.

 TODDLERS

Build on your toddler's passion for labeling everything in her environment with beautifully illustrated word books. Choose word books that categorize objects, such as shape, color, number, or alphabet books. Again, have your child participate by asking her where things are in the illustrations. Wordless story books offer an excellent introduction to stories. Their descriptive illustrations make the story line easy to understand and inviting for toddlers to enjoy on their own. Continue reading rhyme books to strengthen your child's understanding of language structure. Point to the words on the page to show your toddler that the favorite rhymes she knows can be written down for everyone to enjoy and learn. Select picture book stories about toddlers and their world. Share stories about characters, who like your child, are beginning to venture out on their own. Don't be discouraged by a wiggly toddler's limited attention span. Read aloud as along as she is interested, increasing the time by a few minutes each day.

 PRESCHOOLERS

A preschooler will enjoy all of the book types described above, but at a new level of sophistication. Her participation in the read-aloud activity will grow. She may help you read words and refrains from those now familiar rhyme books. And, there will certainly be much discussion about what you read. By now your child has definite interests. Select books together that fascinate your child. Include nonfiction books that respond to her many "why's." Choose picture book stories that offer perspective on her widening world of people, relationships, events, and fantasy. If you began your read-aloud program at birth, your preschooler may even be ready to listen to a daily chapter from a short novel. Try a page and see if your child is interested. *James and the Giant Peach*, by Roald Dahl, *Charlotte's Web* and *Stuart Little* by E. B. White are classics that offer a perfect introduction to novels. Many more favorites can be found in the read-aloud books listed in *Beyond Beginning Reading*, chapter 9, *Treasury*.

 PRIMARY GRADERS

Maintain your role of "book-advocate" for your primary-grade child. Your child is probably receiving formal reading instruction at school. A steady diet of learn-to-read books with simple words and plots can bore a school-age child whose listening comprehension may far exceed her reading ability. Keep up a read-aloud program of challenging literature to assure your child that books are the key to a fascinating world of knowledge, adventure, fantasy, and insight. Choose picture books with sophisticated stories and more text per page. The novels listed above are ideal for primary-grade listeners. Poetry is still important, but now move from nursery rhymes to the hilarious and insightful verses of such poets as Shel Silverstein and Jack Prelutsky. Books with refrains now become read-together books.

Make read-aloud time a special daily experience. Many parents read to their children before bed, an ideal time to cuddle and share a book. Your child has your undivided attention during this calm part of the day as you read a story together. But anytime can be read-aloud time.

Set the stage by warming your child to the book. Guess what it might be about by looking at the cover and title. Talk about her experiences that relate to this book. Now enjoy, as you read aloud!

TRANSFERRING STRATEGIES

Reading strategies you model become those your child will imitate when she reads independently. It's the interaction between you as you share the story, not just the story itself, that makes reading aloud so effective.

 UNDERSTANDING BOOK CONVENTIONS

Use read-aloud time to introduce what a book is all about. Show your child how a book has a front and back. Show how it is read page by page from first page to last. Point out the text and how words are read from the top of the page to the bottom, moving from left to right.

 UNDERSTANDING PRINT CONVENTIONS

Use read aloud time to introduce what print is all about. Show your child how print is made up of individual words, in a particular sequence, that record ideas. We can read those words to enjoy a story or gain information.

 UNDERSTANDING WRITTEN LANGUAGE

Reading aloud is the best way to introduce your child to written language. Although written language is similar to spoken language, it is not the same. Different words, sentences, and structures are used to deliver meaning. Reading aloud familiarizes your child with this new language.

 ASSOCIATING PRINT WITH MESSAGE

Follow along with your finger from time to time as you read. Your child will make the association that this marvelous story comes from these words. She may even associate the particular words you're saying with those you're pointing to.

 EXTENDING VOCABULARY

Your child will hear many new words when you read to her. She learns their meaning through context, just as she does from hearing spoken language. As you read, explain only the words necessary to understand the story. Save the rest for after you finish. Too many unknown words make the story frustrating to listen to. But don't deny your child the rich language of such captivating tales as *Outside Over There* by Maurice Sendak: *arbor, wonder horn, changeling,* and *frenzied.* The detailed pictures and simple rhythmic story help fill the unknown words with meaning.

 HEARING LANGUAGE FLOW

Language must flow to be understood. Its structure must be clear. Remember hearing choppy reading during your school days? The rhythm is uneven and many words must be sounded out. The reader is left with seemingly unrelated words devoid of meaning. When you read, make the words come alive with your voice. Be dramatic, not just to maintain interest in the story, but to better impart the meaning of the text. Let your child hear the beautiful flow of written language read aloud.

UNDERSTANDING STORY ELEMENTS

Talk together about the characters of the story. Who's the hero? (Harry from *Harry, the Dirty Dog* by Gene Zion.) What problem does he face? (He hates taking baths!) How does he solve it? (He hides his bath brush and runs away.) What's the most exciting part or climax of the story? (When Harry comes back home so dirty that the children don't recognize him.) How does he solve this problem? (He finds his brush and lets the children bathe him.)

PREDICTING MEANING

As discussed in chapter 2, good readers intuitively and continually use prediction skills while reading. As we read, we are guessing what will happen next. We continue reading to learn the outcome. Let your child practice prediction skills as you read aloud. Pause during parts of a familiar story to let her fill in the language. Pause at an exciting part in the plot of a new story and ask, "What do you think will happen next?" Encourage her to make logical predictions based on what she already knows of the story and how things occur in her life. Ask, "Why do you think that will happen?" Join in with your own forecasts to model how predictions are made. Then say, "Let's read more to see what will happen." Pausing for predictions helps maintain interest. It also encourages children to draw on their own knowledge and the information they've gleaned from the story. This process is essential to comprehending what we read.

The importance of predicting is in the process. Make this a fun activity for forming logical predictions, not right or wrong answers. Help your child develop a predictive mind set toward print by reading folk tales such as *The Gingerbread Man, The Three Bears,* or *The Little Red Hen.* These predictable stories follow a sequence of events that children pride themselves on being able to guess. Not only are the plots predictable, but often there are repeating phrases that they can predict and read. ("Not I," said the cat. "Not I," said the rat. "Not I," said the pig.) Many modern tales such as Robert Munsch's *Mortimer,* also make use of refrains (see chapter 9. *Treasury*).

ENCOURAGING CREATIVE THINKING SKILLS

As discussed in chapter 2, certain questions encourage creative thinking. Although you may ask a few knowledge and understanding questions to make sure your child is following the story, focus on creative thinking questions that stimulate your child to use information for problem solving and other creative endeavors: "What would happen if you woke up and found you had shrunk? How would your day be different from George's?" (*George Shrinks*) "How are George's problems different from Imogene's? The same?" (*Imogene's Antlers*) "Let's write a letter for the *Jolly Postman* to deliver from the cat to the *Little Red Hen.*" "Suppose Jimmy had a pet monkey instead of a boa. How would the field trip have been different?" "What if the boa had escaped at the beach instead of a farm. What might have happened?" (*The Day Jimmy's Boa Ate the Wash*) "How can you tell this story is make-believe?" "What would you do if . . ." "Was what s/he did right? Why do you think so?"

INSTILLING AN INTEREST IN BOOKS

Engage in "book-talk" not only while you read aloud, but at other times of day. "What did you think of the ending to *Where the Wild Things Are?*" Use books as reference points: "I feel like the bull Ferdinand today. I just want to lie in the backyard and smell the flowers." Or, "Let's eat lunch like the *Very Hungry Caterpillar* ate his."

 ## APPLYING READING TO LIFE

Enliven stories by relating their content to your personal lives. While sharing Peter Spier's *Rain* ask, "When you went out in the rain today, what discoveries did you make?" Or, "If you were *The Giving Tree*, would you give the boy all you had?" "How would you feel if your toy bear was lost?" "What would you do if you could fly?" "What did you see when you looked in the tall grass at the park?"

All experiences — those she has herself and those she reads about — enhance comprehension. You'll increase her awareness of reality and fantasy about her world and other worlds. And you'll help make reading a vital part of her life.

 ## BRIDGING INDEPENDENCE

Fulfill those requests to hear the same book dozens of times. Repeated readings familiarize your child with its many aspects. Favorite read-aloud books, especially those with predictable language or plots, are particularly helpful in allowing her to retell the story.

Children model reading by retelling a familiar story while turning the pages. They participate in reading as an enjoyable activity. Research suggests that repeated retellings may be the roots of independent reading and indeed actually promote high achievement. Encourage your child to "read" by retelling books you've read aloud. It not only develops her self-concept as a reader, it's a crucial first step in becoming one.

By reading aloud you can impart an understanding for what written language is all about, how to make sense of it, and its value. The value of reading aloud for eventual reading success is widely recognized.

CREATING A LITERACY-RICH HOME

Develop a "literacy-rich lifestyle" where reading material makes its way into every aspect of your child's life. Keep books, pads, and pens in your car. Tiny editions of favorite books are available for your purse. Books even make good bathroom companions. Install a light above your child's bed to encourage the literacy-building habit of reading in bed. If your child is dining alone, set down a magazine near her breakfast. Do set aside daily time to read aloud, but also set aside quiet time for your child to read through an appealing pile of books, alone. Silently turning pages or retelling a tale aloud are the beginning forms of independent reading your child needs to practice.

Involve your child in some sort of daily writing, perhaps writing out a shopping or to-do list together, or you or your child writing down some of her ideas in a diary or journal. Let your child catch you in the act of reading and writing as part of your literacy-rich lifestyle.

Create a home library where your child can access books easily. Books are now widely available for every interest and ability level. Include a variety of picture books, predictable stories, those you've read aloud, poetry, alphabet books, nonfiction, and catalogs. Include books you and your child have made (see chapter 7). Expand her library with gifts and used books. Add your child's very own magazine subscription. And don't forget the public library's invaluable collection. Plan regular trips, and as soon as she can write her name, outfit your child with her own precious library card.

Create a well-stocked, pint-sized office filled with the pens, paper, and supplies she needs to compose messages, make pictures, or author books (see *Office, Activities*, chapter 6).

Add manipulative literacy materials, such as alphabet blocks and puzzles to her toy shelf.

Invent reasons for using written language. Even beginning readers love receiving printed messages. Just add picture clues or read them aloud. Note future events on a large calendar: *Jessica's birthday party October 17 at 3:00.* Label toy shelves and drawers for their contents: pajamas, trucks, dolls. Install a blackboard or marker board in the kitchen or other family area. List the dinner menu or reminders on the blackboard: *Library books due today.* Set up a family bulletin board where messages and reminders can be pinned. Write a note to your child reminding her to pick up her toys or come to lunch. Include a note in her lunch box: *Dear Jenna, Have a good time at school. Love, Mom.* Add a food list or tape food labels on to baggies, labeling their contents. Share information on packaging, instruction manuals, the TV listing. Include your child in reading advertising that is relevant to her. "Look, it says that the circus is coming to town!" Or, while pointing to the ad say, "There's the movie you've been wanting to see." Then read the details aloud as you follow along with your finger. If you have an excuse to communicate in print, do it!

COMPUTERS

Get ready to read. Find an old, soft chair and curl up with— a computer? Although it doesn't sound too cozy, children's stories are now available on CD-ROM Disc in very enticing formats. Also, there are learn-to-read software programs where words, letters, and comical characters dance about on a full-color screen. Computers offer unlimited skill practice. Operation of the computer provides opportunities for functional reading of such commands as *file, edit, delete*, and so on. The "teacher" is very patient and can be completely nonjudgmental.

Although a traditionalist may fault learn-to-read software for being nothing more than video-workbooks, new technologies are here to stay and will play an increasingly important role in your child's future. Rather than debate the relative superiority of the printed word to the electronic word, accept the electronic word as the vital form of communication that it is. Offer your child computer access along with opportunities to explore all forms of written language. You can give your child access to your word processing program. Just set the point size at about 18 and let her peck away.

Purchasing specially designed software for children is worth looking into. No one can deny the appeal of animated "talking" programs that invite a child to play — and learn. (See chapter 9, the *Treasury* for critically acclaimed software and parent guides that evaluate programs.)

Select computer software with the same care you'd select any other educational material or toy for your child. We have already discussed how children learn best through self-directed, interactive learning (see *How Children Learn*, chapter 2). Does the software allow for such learning? Here are some criteria to look for.

SELF-DIRECTED LEARNING

The software should allow children to choose from a variety of activities. Children should be able to easily and independently access and quit activities when they choose.

 OPEN-ENDED, INTERACTIVE EXPLORATION

Instead of drill formats, look for software that allows children to experiment and make judgments as a way to solve problems.

 EDUCATIONAL VALUE

The skill presented should be worth learning. The content should be high quality. Ideally, programs offer a variety of topics or a range of exploration possibilities within a topic.

 MULTI-LEVEL LEARNING

Concept exploration should be possible at a variety of levels. Choose software that adapts to the child's growing knowledge, allowing her to learn a skill, apply it, then move on to a new skill. The activities should be doable independently, without being boring. They should challenge, yet not be frustrating. Some programs automatically adjust the degree of difficulty based on the child's performance.

 OPPORTUNITIES FOR SUCCESS

Programs should encourage risk-taking through trial and error, as a way to solve problems. The software should guide children to the right answer through feedback that avoids the connotation that errors are wrong answers.

 FUN AND ATTRACTIVE

The activities should be entertaining, imaginative, and engaging. The graphics should be attractive and appealing.

When all of the above criteria are in place, your child will enjoy and benefit from computer time!

FUNCTIONAL READING

Don't be afraid to use print when communicating with your beginning reader. Even if she cannot yet read the words, she needs to see firsthand how print carries important meaning. Supplement printed messages with picture clues and/or read the messages aloud, so she can participate in receiving print communication. Also, encourage your beginning writer to respond with scribbles, pictures, or pretend writing, so she can continue to participate in the process of using written language.

 I CAN READ BOOK

This personalized book is filled with the environmental print your child already reads so successfully. On each page, fill in the blank with the word your child can read: I can read *McDonald's*. Illustrate the page by pasting beneath the sentence the part of the packaging or magazine ad that displays the word. If you choose a word from a sign, draw a picture of that sign: I can read *stop*, illustrated with a stop sign. (See page 156 for activity materials.)

 LABEL RECALL

Cut brand names from two identical labels of household products. Paste them on index cards. When you have about ten pairs of cards, you can play *Match, Recall,* and *Pairs* (see *Activities,* chapter 5).

 WORD CONTEST

Which word is more frequently seen from her car seat, stop or exit? Help her find out by printing the words at the top of an index card. Draw a line between them and she can keep score by tallying beneath the word at each sighting. The word with the most tallies when the trip ends wins! Any words likely to be seen on a walk or shopping cart tour can compete. Or, simply have your child call out the word each time she sees it.

 MAIL

Let your child decorate 9" x 12" envelopes to create simple mailboxes. Label them *Ashley's Mailbox* and *Mommy's* or *Daddy's Mailbox* and tape them to bedroom doors. Send letters back and forth. Encourage all forms of writing: letter shapes, single words, phrases, and pictures.

SECRET MESSAGES

Hide messages around the house for your child to find and read. Write them on slips of paper, then fold and write her name on the outside. Add picture clues or be prepared to read the message aloud to the beginning reader. While she's playing before lunch time, hand her a message that says, "To Morgan, It's time for lunch. Love, Mom." Write messages on a chalkboard to each other. Secret messages prove that print is functional. Children love to solve mysteries.

 SCAVENGER HUNT

Send your child on a search for odds and ends around your home. Equip her with a list of treasures to find and a bag in which to carry the bounty: *2 rocks, 3 sticks, 1 leaf. . . .* Remember to add pictures of the items for beginning readers.

 TREASURE HUNT

Hide a toy somewhere in your home. Leave a series of notes to help your child find them. For example, start with a note stating, "Go to the kitchen table." On the kitchen table have another note ready stating, "Go to your bed." There your child finds a note directing her to another location. She'll continue finding and following instructions on notes until she's located her toy. For beginning readers, add pictures of each location.

 MADISON AVENUE

Writing needn't be lengthy or always in story form. It's fun to write short, functional messages or make drawings for greeting cards, posters, bumper stickers, or T-shirts. Older children can even design an original product and create an advertisement for it.

CREATING A LITERACY–RICH HOME

"ME" SCRAPBOOK

What could make more fascinating reading than a book about your child? Make one by providing her with a blank scrapbook, spiral-bound sketch pad, or binder filled with sheets of heavy-weight paper. Next, have her gather those postcards, ticket stubs, programs, birthday cards, leaves, and other souvenirs and paste them into her scrapbook. Encourage her to write or draw about events. Date each entry. She can add photos, jokes, songs, and descriptions of friends and events to make this a potpourri of treasured memories.

AUDIO RECORDINGS

Commercial audio recordings expose your child to the finest children's literature read aloud by outstanding actors and actresses. Or make your own recordings of the favorite stories requested again and again. Let your child show off her budding ability by reading or telling stories into a tape recorder. Create an anthology with contributions from visitors who come to your home: readings of stories and poems by friends and relatives or Grandpa's favorite yarns.

FOLK TALE FUN

Folk tales embody cultural and literary themes so universal that similar versions can be found in almost every country and culture. *Goldilocks, Three Billy Goats Gruff, Gingerbread Man, The Three Little Pigs*, and *The Little Red Hen* should be "required reading" for all children. Seek out several versions from different storytellers or countries. How are they alike? Different? Together create your own versions. "One day while we were out shopping and letting our hamburgers cool, a little bear came into our house..." Here are other ways to extend the magic of folk tales or any story. Some of these activities will require your help. Your child can:

- Role play a conversation between characters
- Interview one of the characters
- Illustrate her favorite part
- Come up with a new ending
- Act out the story or an original version with costumes, puppets and/or sound effects
- Cook up a food from the story such as stone soup or a gingerbread man
- Make a map of where the action took place
- Make up a musical ballad of the tale
- Retell the tale in a present-day setting.

LITERARY ART

Extend your child's understanding and enjoyment of stories through art. Let her illustrate her favorite stories. She can make paper bag puppets or masks of characters, then use them to dramatize the story. She can recreate favorite scenes and characters with paint, pens, or clay.

LOVE COUPONS

The perfect gift! Let your child see how important print can be by making and redeeming valuable coupons. On one side of the coupon, each of you describe something special to do for the other. Illustrate the activity on the backside. For your child, you could offer to: *Read a book* or *Play a game*. By communicating through pictures and/or words, your child can make love coupons for you to redeem: *A hug; Clean up;* or *No fighting for a year*. Preschool teachers take note. Love coupons make an ideal Mother's Day gift. (See page 160 for activity materials.)

STORYTELLING

You can spin a tale anytime, anyplace. Enliven a long trip for your bored passenger by sharing a bit of family history or a favorite story from your childhood. Or, tell a tale with your child as the hero. Model storytelling, and your child will soon be inspired to create her own yarns.

FAST FOOD FUN

Make a trip for a burger into a "reading outing." With your guidance, invite your child to read the road signs along the way. As you approach the restaurant, let your child call out it's name and then read the sign to see if it's open or closed. Point out how food is categorized on the menu board: sandwiches, beverages, desserts. When the food arrives, read the packaging to figure out what's inside. Reading fun can continue back home. Save all packaging, receipts, paper placemats, and so on for your child to set up her own make-believe "Burger World." Follow the same steps to make any outing into a reading outing. The post office or bank are perfect with their many signs and forms. Gather tags, receipts, coupons, and printed bags from a trip to the store.

FIELD EXPLORER

Outfit your young explorer with a small pad of paper or a clipboard. Invite her to record a day's adventures. She might jot notes or draw pictures of the post office or store. She can find things to observe and note right in her own backyard. Another possibility is to keep notes and drawings documenting the progress of a captured bug or a growing seed. Date her entries and treat them as exciting scientific data.

 AT-HOME LITERACY

The following is a summary and review of the many ways you can share literacy as a natural part of daily life.

- Referring to recipes while cooking
- Copying and filing favorite family recipes
- Referring to manuals for carpentry, gardening, etc.
- Referring to instructions when assembling toys or playing games
- Reading travel schedules and entertainment guides
- Maintaining a family diary, travel log, or scrapbook
- Labeling the photos in a family photo album
- Updating a family calendar with special events, birthdays, and appointments

- Entering information in the address book
- Writing out shopping, trip-packing, and to-do lists
- Addressing, signing, and mailing Christmas cards and Valentines
- Making and sending original get well, thank you, invitation, and birthday cards
- Writing letters and postcards to friends and relatives
- Cutting out, filing, and using coupons
- Pointing out interesting ads, photos, and articles in newspapers and magazines
- Singing songs and telling stories while on trips
- Pointing out environmental print at home and on outings
- Writing messages and reminders to each other
- Referring to maps, travel brochures, and guides while on trips
- Creating an inviting, well-stocked home library and writing area
- Installing and using a chalkboard, marker board, and/or bulletin board
- Making read-aloud, reading-alone, and writing a regular part of everyday
- Making time for all family members to enjoy books, magazines, and newspapers on their own.

CHAPTER 5

Reading Special Words & Language

USING YOUR CHILD'S OWN WORDS FOR LEARNING

LEARNING TO READ IS LIKE LEARNING TO LISTEN

By reading aloud and by sharing printed lyrics of favorite songs, children are exposed to written language in its most complete form. These beginning reading experiences with whole language are like first listening experiences in which children are immersed in conversation with an adult.

Listen carefully to language directed toward a beginning speaker. Not only are whole sentences used, but important words are repeated and emphasized to help him understand and repeat the word. "Do you want a cookie? Cookie . . . cookie?" And what would you expect him to say next time he craves sweets? "Cookie!" This single word contains whole meaning for that child.

When he says "cookie!" the parent's natural response is to fill in the missing language. "Oh, you want a cookie. We have oatmeal cookies today." And so the conversation continues with repeated shifting between emphasizing and isolating important words, and then putting those words back into the whole language context of purposeful speech by the adult. Your child can learn to read words the same way he learned to say them. His first spoken words were of great personal importance. With careful selection, the first words he learns to read can also be those of great personal importance. These first words will continually be fed back into the whole language context of sentences, songs, and books.

THE IMPORTANCE OF A WORD

As we've discussed, individual words can carry whole meaning: A mother cradles her baby while repeating, "Mama, mama, mama." She rejoices when she hears a similar response and the baby soon equates "mama" with mom. This simple sound holds a world of meaning and the baby learns the power of a word.

A toddler points his finger everywhere and an excited little voice shouts, "Tree!" "Dog!" "What's that?" His appetite for words is insatiable. The single word "shoes" can mean, "Help me put my shoes on. I want to come along, too!" "What

does that mean?" becomes a constant question as a child's language keeps pace with his growing intellect.

In an environment filled with billboards, shop names, and street signs, individual words carry important meaning. Just as the whole language of a song is significant to a child, so are individual words, when learned in a meaningful context. Your child first learned to say *swing, slide,* and *sandbox* on an outing to the park. Similarly, he'll learn to read such words while he's encountering firsthand what they represent.

WHAT ARE SIGHT WORDS?

Sight words are those we identify by their appearance. Language must flow to be understood. If every word is sounded out, meaning is lost. So to avoid stopping to figure out each word, the reader must have a huge storehouse of those he recognizes immediately.

Learning to read sight words also sensitizes children to their function as distinct sub-units of language. When we speak, we flow words together without pausing between them. When we write, we separate words with spaces so they can be easily rearranged to create different meanings.

READY TO LEARN SIGHT WORDS

A good indication that your child is ready to learn sight words is when he begins to ask, "What does that say?" But the best indicator is his interest in learning them. Keep an open mind as you teach your child sight words, following the procedure described here. Teach one word at a time. If he's interested, continue. If not, wait until he is. Some toddlers enjoy seeing their name, *Mommy,* or *Fido* printed on

a card. They love to carry a word card around, then leave it among their toys, treating it with the same respect they give to any found treasure. On the other hand, some preschoolers have no patience or interest in seeing printed word cards. So drop the activity for now, trying it again from time to time. Remember, you are offering *opportunities* for your child to freely explore written language.

CHOOSING SPECIAL WORDS

Every child has a unique vocabulary. Children learn and favor particular words. Let the words your child loves to say be the first sight words he learns to read. We'll call these "special words."

Begin by picking three favorites. If *dinosaur, Big Bird, pizza,* or any other words have special importance, use those. The words must be charged with meaning. Although words such as *the, are,* and *was* are considered "easy" words found in typical beginning reading books, they are actually difficult for your child to learn because they lack exciting meaning.

Also, be sure the three words are easily differentiated. *Mommy, Tommy,* and *monster* may be confused due to their similar sounds, length, and overall appearance. *Matthew, hamburger,* and *zoo* invite success because each word sounds and looks unique.

Using a felt-tip marker, print the first special word on a card. Cards are easily made from horizontal quarter-sheets of standard 8 1/2" x 11" blank index card stock available at stationery stores or print shops. Card stock is recommended because the word cards will be used again and again. Capitalize the first letter only if appropriate, such as in a proper name. See *Sentence springboards* on page 162 for approximate letter form and card size.

LEARNING THE FIRST SPECIAL WORD

Give your child opportunities to experience the special words in meaningful contexts: hug him as he learns *hug;* show him *jump* while he's jumping; or share his favorite *dinosaur* story before learning dinosaur. These special word cards become personalized billboards celebrating the word and what's special to him.

As an example, we'll choose the word *pretzel.* Food words are excellent choices because they arouse vivid memories of pleasant sensory experiences. While he munches on one, show the word and say, "This word is *pretzel.*" While he watches, repeat "pretzel" following under the word with your finger. Always use an expressive voice and be enthusiastic as you say the word to make this a vivid learning experience. Put the card down and continue your discussion about pretzels for about half a minute.

Show the word two more times, pronouncing it enthusiastically each time. Leave the card near a left-over pretzel as an in-house billboard "advertising" the word and what it represents. If handy, also show your child the word pretzel on the package it came in.

Presenting a single word a few times, interspersed with play or discussion, is called a *word presentation.* Make several word presentations with the same word throughout the course of the day and taking no more than three minutes each time.

You needn't provide a snack each time your child sees the word. Simply remind him of the event. At the beginning of each presentation, give him a moment to read the word. Then quickly say it if he doesn't respond. He may read the word aloud after one showing or many. Remember how often your baby heard you say "mama" before he said the word.

Even when he responds correctly, continue providing opportunities to read the word (see *Reviewing the Words* on page 66). Now your child can read a word that is special to him!

LEARNING ADDITIONAL WORDS

Teach the second special word as you did the first. Remember to choose a word that looks very different from the first. Now your child must learn that not all print says pretzel (or whatever word you chose to present). Let him differentiate between the first two special words before learning more. Some children take this step with ease, while others need more time.

When he can read the second word, review it and teach the third special word in the same way. Offer only as many word presentations as he needs to learn the word.

If your child wants to learn more special words, great! Continue to expand his sight vocabulary as described and whenever he is interested. Creating contexts for learning

these words is simple when word selection grows from your child's interests, experiences, and language. Simply present *towel* during a daily wash-up or jot down *pinecone* reminding him of the discovery made on your walk.

Read-aloud books create contexts for learning many new words: *Carrot, seed, nothing,* and *grow* are all from Ruth Krauss's *The Carrot Seed. Hungry, bubbled, juicy,* and *barley* are from Ann McGovern's version of *Stone Soup.*

As he becomes a more experienced sight-word reader, drop the card size. You can use 3" x 5" index cards, the backs of business cards, and eventually business cards cut into quarters.

REVIEWING THE WORDS

While continuing to present new words, review the learned ones during spare moments throughout the day. Use your imagination to provide fast-and-fun practice.

- Leave the word next to the object it names.
- Seal a word card in an envelope and "deliver" it as an important message.
- Let your child read the words to a puppet or favorite toy.
- Place a word card on his empty plate at mealtime. Say, "Look, there's your word. What does it say?" Word cards can appear leaning against the television set, on the car seat, in the toy box, or hidden around the house. Like so many stuffed animals, the words become friends.
- Spread word cards across the floor and give fun instructions to follow, such as, "Hop to the word *Mommy*. Put your toy dog on *dog*. Put *girl* on the chair."
- Offer a word card to read to Dad or Mom in the next room. Children delight in taking words back and forth between parents, reading, and being applauded for their efforts.

- Keep a small set of word cards in your pocket or purse to use while spending time in lines, restaurants, or waiting rooms.
- Keep word cards magnetized to the refrigerator or in any handy place where they'll be read.
- Point out familiar words in books you read aloud.
- Place a chalk or marker board at a height accessible to your child in a place where you're often together. Write review words on the board for him to read or illustrate.
- Use chalk to write monstrous words on your driveway. Let your child walk, hop, tip-toe, or bike along the letters as he chants the word.
- Make a book of words pertaining to a particular topic. For example, *What I Can Do* would have a page for each word such as *jump, run, climb,* and an illustration by your child. *Summer* might feature *beach, swim, hot,* and *sun* (see chapter 7, *Creating Books*).

LEARNING TO READ SENTENCES

Learning to read special words sparks your child's word recognition ability. However, just as he learns most words through conversation, so will he learn to read most words independently through the course of his reading. Unknown words in print become meaningful to him when he brings his knowledge of the content and language to the page. So he needs plenty of exposure to the "conversation" of sentences, songs, and stories for this to occur. The following phrases provide a structure on which to "hang" special words: I love —; I can —; I eat —; Hello —. We'll call these *sentence springboards*. The sentences and phrases you generate with them allow comfortable reading of his special words in a whole language context.

When sentence springboards are repeatedly combined with special words, the resulting sentences are so meaningful he reads them intuitively. For example, lay out *I love* (use *Sentence springboards* on page 162) and a special word card such as *Mommy* edge to edge to form *I love Mommy*.

Read this sentence together. Then create more sentences following this pattern by substituting a new special word card: *I love spaghetti; I love Daddy; I love dinosaurs.*

Although your child learned to sequence events, he needs your support in applying this skill to reading words. He must learn that printed words are written in a particular sequence that corresponds with the order in which they are spoken. Place your finger beneath each word to direct his eyes from left to right as he reads.

Now he's read a sentence! He can also read sentences following this pattern: *Hello, Mommy; Hello, Grandpa; Hello, Matthew.* With *eat*, he can read *I eat pizza, giraffes eat leaves, birds eat insects. Can* enables him to read: *I can swim; Mommy can climb; Bats can fly.* As more special words are learned, use them to create new sentences.

By reading sentences, he experiences how words come together to produce expanded meaning. The songs and books he reads will show him how sentences combine to create new orders of meaning beyond individual sentences.

I love	Mommy

race cars

tomatoes

LET'S SING

Do you remember this song from summer camp?

> *I love the mountains.*
> *I love the rolling hills.*
> *I love the flowers.*
> *I love the daffodils.*
> *I love the fireside*
> *When all the lights are low.*
> *Boom de ah duh*
> *Boom de ah duh*
> *Boom de ah duh*
> *Boom de ah duh*
> *Boom, boom, boom*

Together, read and sing from the song sheet, *I Love the Mountains* (see page 163 for activity materials). It reinforces the new sentence pattern he's just learned. Since the word *the* is structural and sounds right in the song, there's no need to present it as a new word. Simply point to it and read it as casually as any other word on the page. Do not teach structural words such as *the, to,* or *on* through word presentations or you will bore your child. It is fine to just go ahead and use them as needed for creating sentences.

Now create an original version using your child's special words. Don't hesitate to add words or make special words plural to make the song more rhythmic or meaningful. You can make an original song sheet to read together or just enjoy the language of the silly song.

> *I love spaghetti.*
> *I love well-done steak.*
> *I love tortillas.*
> *I love chocolate cake.*
> *I love tuna fish*
> *When all the food is fresh.*
> *Munch and crunch*
> *And chomp and chew*
> *And munch and crunch*
> *And chomp and chew*

Once comfortable with the *I love* sentence pattern, your child is ready to read the *First Reading Book* entitled, *I Love* (see Activity Materials, page 165).

PREPARING **I LOVE** FOR READING

As with *1, 2!*, the principle of familiarity is used in *I Love* to assure success. The vocabulary consists of your child's special words. The repetitive phrase pattern helps him predict the words, and the large print is easy to read.

On each printed page, add one of your child's special words beneath the phrase *I love.* Go ahead and add structural words such as *to* or *the* as they are needed to form natural-sounding sentences.

On the first page, you may wish to write your child's name. Use a black felt-tip marker and print in lower-case letters, capitalizing only the first letters of proper nouns. Approximate the form and size of the pre-printed text.

On the facing page, paste a family or magazine photograph or a drawing by you or your child to illustrate the sentence. Use our format to make as many pages as you like: *I love Grandma; I love tyrannosaurs; I love pepperoni.* A personalized book makes meaningful and motivational reading material.

LET'S READ *I LOVE*

The variety of early reading experiences you offer strengthens your child's reading ability. By reading and reciting lyrics of familiar songs and the refrains of predictable stories, he has become a full-fledged participant in the reading process (see *Reading Whole Language,* page 39).

Your repeated readings of favorite books have encouraged your child to independently retell these same stories. This independent "reading" of real books builds his self-image as a reader (see *Bridging independence,* page 52).

Now your child will delight in reading a book personalized with his own favorite words. With your child cozy on your lap, joyfully say, "Here's a book you can read all by yourself!" Point to the title and let him read, "*I Love.*" Talk for a few moments together about what the book's subject might be.

Now open the book to the first page. Guide his eyes from left to right by moving your finger beneath *I love* to his name. Enthusiastically reinforce correct reading by declaring, "Yes, it says, 'I love Eric,' and there you are!"

Fill the print with meaning by relating it to his world: "I love to swim . . . . Remember swimming in Grandma's pool? You swam all day and made so many friends." Your child's imagination far exceeds his reading ability. So help fill the gap by discussing the page, making it interesting and relevant.

If he needs help reading this or any other new material encountered, here are suggestions:

- Have your child read after your lively reading of the phrase, paragraph, or selection.
- Call attention to repeating phrases and picture clues.
- You read as he points to each word. Now you point as he reads.
- Read aloud together, letting him lead whenever possible.

Just as repeated read-aloud and story retelling experiences benefit your child, so does repeated independent reading. Reading a story again and again is the best practice for improving fluency, accuracy, comprehension, and oral reading expression. Repeated reading helps him glean more information and deeper meaning from the text.

Your child's reading experiences have now come full circle. He's experienced whole language through the books you've read aloud and the songs you've sung and read together. He's also read his own words and watched them flow together into that same whole language of familiar songs and books. He can read *I Love* on his own. Success will inspire him to read other books you create (see chapter 7) and "real" books (see chapters 8 and 9). He's well on his way to becoming a confident reader!

CELEBRATING SPECIAL WORDS

SPECIAL WORD CARDS

Create a duplicate set of word or picture cards to match his special words. Match word to word or word to picture. Let's assume you're matching word to picture cards in these examples.

 MATCH

Spread out a few picture cards. Have him place a word card beneath the corresponding picture. When he can match these few, increase the number. Vary this game by spreading out word cards first.

 RECALL

For a greater challenge, spread all cards face down in rows. Turn over two at a time. If they match, keep the pair and take another turn. If not, turn the cards face down again. Play noncompetitively by taking turns finding pairs.

 PAIRS

Deal the cards between you until all are distributed. Set aside pairs within your hand. Now let your child draw a card from your hand. If it matches a card in his, set the pair aside. Take turns until all pairs are matched.

WORD SCRAPBOOK

Create a scrapbook filled with unique words and illustrations clipped from magazines and packaging, or your child's own drawings. Use 8 1/2" x 11" sheets of construction paper for each page. Punch holes along the side of each page and store them in a binder. Make this an ongoing activity.

COME TO THE CIRCUS

Stack word cards face down. Tape numerals 2 and 3 on opposite sides of a penny. Use buttons as playing pieces and place them on Start. Have your child pick up a card. If he can read the word, he can toss the penny and move as many spaces as indicated. Replace the cards at the bottom of the stack. If he lands on a space with written directions, help him read and follow them. Take turns until you both *Come to the Circus*. (See page 173 for activity materials.)

WORDS EVERYWHERE

Create mini-billboards for your home. Lean *apple*, *juice*, and *cookie* cards against these foods at snack time. Place *Teddy bear* in the stuffed toy's lap or tape *Kara's room* on her bedroom door. Together you can label furniture, belongings, body parts, and even pets and people. Post-it-Notes™ work great because they fall off just about the time your child loses interest and stops "seeing" the word. Replace with new labels for new items.

WORD LINK-UP

Let your child compose original sentences by laying special words out in a line. The sillier the sentence, the more fun it is to read. Supply him with new cards for needed words. Your child may want to make his own word cards. Take turns making sentences for the other person to read. *A fat yellow pig eats crunchy cucumbers.*

WORD BANK

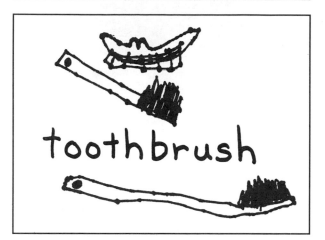

Present your child with a card file box complete with letter or subject dividers. Help him organize his growing word collection by filing his special words alphabetically or by subject categories (*toys, body parts, actions*). He may enjoy decorating cards for special entries.

CHARADES

Write special words that can be acted out on index cards. Players take turns picking these cards from a paper bag and acting them out. The other players guess the word. A variation is to have the player draw a picture of the word while other players guess the word.

WORD SETS

Build vocabulary about favorite subjects. Dinosaurs, anyone? *Stegosaurus, diplodocus, tyrannosaurus.* How about foods? *Mushrooms, ice cream, strawberries.* He can make matching picture cards for each word. Punch a hole in the corner of each card and hold the set together with a metal binder ring. After he has several sets, take them apart and shuffle all cards. Now let him sort the cards back into their original or new categories.

WORD COLLAGE

Increase your child's vocabulary through art. Make a decorative poster celebrating favorite words or concepts. Together hunt through magazine ads for high-impact words and pictures relating to a particular word or concept, for example, *happy*. Clip and paste what you find (*joy, delight, cheer, gay,* and photos of happy faces) onto bright paper. Or, freely cut and paste any attractive words or pictures onto poster paper.

CHAPTER 6

Writing

COMMUNICATING IDEAS
THROUGH PRINT

WRITING IS COMMUNICATING

When we read, we receive ideas and information from print. When we write, we transmit our own ideas and knowledge through print. Just as getting meaning must be the driving force behind learning to read, generating meaning must be the driving force behind learning to write. Children need to perceive writing as a powerful tool for communicating their own important ideas, if they are to become proficient and enthusiastic writers. What kind of writing experiences promote the value of writing? Certainly not tedious letter formation drills. Such drills are an imposition on the beginning writer and actually hinder the process. They do nothing to convince children that writing is communication. Encouraging children to convey their own vital messages in print is the most meaningful writing experience you can offer. That experience begins not with the first time your child tries to copy a word, but with the first scribbles your baby makes.

STAGES OF WRITING DEVELOPMENT

Just like learning to speak, writing follows a natural progression from random to refined. Children reinvent the writing process through their own experimentation over time. The driving force seems to be the power children achieve from leaving their mark, especially when their writing is recognized as valuable by the important people in their lives. If children are focused on generating meaning, they will naturally strive for accuracy and be motivated to learn the necessary skills to convey their important messages. The following stages of development take place over several years.

Writing begins with the first attempts to make meaningful marks. This early scribbling compares with the babbling language-play babies engage in before they talk. Coos, babbles, and cries are real communication and so are scribbles.

Just as babbling soon sounds more like words, random scribbling becomes more controlled, and uniform strokes and shapes are formed. Next, recognizable drawings emerge.

Eventually letter-like scribbles appear mixed with drawings in an effort to communicate in print. While a blank sheet of paper may inspire a drawing, a lined sheet may result in rows and rows of strokes resembling cursive or manuscript writing. Next, strings of seemingly random letters are produced.

Children immersed in a print-rich environment sense that writing needs to be composed of real letters and words in order for their message to be understood. This sense motivates them to upgrade their "pretend" letters and words into "real" ones in order to make meaningful messages.

Children seek knowledge of letter sounds and formation when they realize spelling words is a better way to have their messages understood. Initially, the first letter sound represents an entire word. Next an awareness of the end sound develops so that *dg* represents *dog*. Later come consonants and vowels in the middle of the word so that *tigr* might represent *tiger*. Children invent word spellings based on their beginning knowledge of letter sounds.

The stages of writing described are by no means absolute. Just as speech becomes refined with opportunities to hear and use it, writing gradually becomes conventional, as children gain more experience reading and putting written language to use. The best learn-to-write materials you can offer at any stage are a wide variety of papers and writing implements. Such open-ended writing material allows multi-ability exploration.

A mix of letters, letter-like shapes, scribbles, and drawings is common in beginning writing.

PROMOTING WRITING

Children must be immersed in written language and have ample opportunities to put it to use, if they are to be successful readers and writers. Chapter 4, *Valuing Reading*, could also have been entitled *Valuing Writing*, because reading and writing are intrinsically related. The ways children can experience the value of written language, discussed in that chapter, will make them successful readers as well as writers: modeling the use of written language; helping children use written language to function in life; reading aloud; and providing a print-rich home. In addition to promoting the value of written language, these activities give children meaningful examples from which to model their own writing.

Child senses a need to add lines to blank paper when writing.

The following are more ways to assure that your child will not just be *able* to write, but will *want* to write:

 PROVIDE AMPLE WRITING OPPORTUNITIES

Children need plenty of experience holding a pen or pencil and drawing freely on blank paper to initiate the natural writing progression described above. Invite your child to experiment with written language. Offer her blank, unlined paper. Do not burden her with the chore of confining her scribbles or letters within neat spaces, unless she is an experienced writer or she requests lined paper. Then, offer paper with lines no more than approximately 1/2" apart, or your child will be forced to draw instead of write letters.

 PROVIDE THE "WRITE" STUFF

Start your baby out with crayons and paper at her high chair. At this age, however, crayons are more fun to eat than draw with, so *you'll need to supervise*. The easiest tool for young writers to use is a marking pen. Very little pressure is needed and the resulting strokes are dazzling. Let your child use what she finds most comfortable and enjoyable. Usually adult-sized writing implements are best. A thick children's pencil is too large for small hands. Set up a well-stocked "office" for your budding writer, filled with writing supplies too much fun to resist (see *Office* on page 89).

**MAKE WRITING
AN INTEGRAL PART OF LIFE**

Your child needs proof that writing is vital communication. She needs to observe you writing: jotting down notes, writing shopping and to-do lists, writing letters and reports. Help her write labels for toy shelves, messages to friends, reminders on the marker board, and notes to you. Encourage writing during imaginative play. Help your young shopkeeper create *Open* and *Closed* signs. Give your police officer a pad and pencil for writing out tickets. As a waitress, she needs an order pad and a chalk board for daily specials. Children value writing when they understand *why* people write.

 ENCOURAGE DRAWING

In addition to its artistic value, this expressive activity allows children to record ideas in a way similar to writing. Beginning writers often enjoy drawing a picture before writing to serve as a rough draft. In fact, many beginners perceive their drawing as actual writing, so be sensitive to their view. Write labels and captions for her drawings, if your child requests them. These become special words she may attempt to copy. She'll use your letters as models to reshape her own letter-like scribbles.

 TALK WITH YOUR CHILD

Writers must have something to say. So to prepare your child for writing, encourage her to talk. If she's at a loss for ideas, discuss a recent experience you've shared. Encourage an outpouring of ideas and language as described under the heading, *Listening and Talking*, page 36. Invite your child to write about anything she likes. Or, use the suggested topics in chapter 7, *Creating Books*.

 **BE AN AUDIENCE FOR
YOUR CHILD'S WRITING**

Remember, as your child progresses through each stage of writing development, she is conveying ideas. So she needs someone to receive those ideas. She may "read" pretend writing to you. Support her budding ability and desire to communicate in print by being an enthusiastic listener. Ask your child to read to you what she has written. Ask her specific questions about the ideas she is trying to convey. Treat all writing (pictures, scribbles, letters, word fragments, words, sentences, or paragraphs) as the valid communication that it is, just as you did the earliest attempts to verbalize.

> I Love ♡ my home. Thers papr and puzls and Kots and musik and tap cusęts and 2 bath roms.

I love my home. There's paper and puzzles and coats and music and tape cassettes and two bathrooms.

WRITING YOUR CHILD'S WORDS

Reading aloud to your child gives her the power of possessing reading ability long before she is able to read on her own. Similarly, writing down your child's words lets her experience this powerful communication tool long before she can write on her own. By acting as a scribe for your child, you model exactly how written language is used, with your child's own words, right before her eyes. The activity proves that the words we say can be written down. Whether it's a label on a picture, a message to Grandma, or a few sentences about going to a birthday party, you're giving her words and thoughts great importance by writing and reading them. She actively communicates through print, even before she's able to write.

The following is a description of how to write a *language experience story* with your child. A language experience story is always preceded by an experience and by oral language. Then the child dictates her story to a scribe who records her words. To start, encourage your child's language to flow. Discuss a favorite event or activity using the techniques outlined in *Listening and Talking*, page 36. Then write her words while she watches you. Be sure to let your child know that you are recording her words as another way of writing, not because she is unable to write. Here's an example of how to begin after you've talked together about an outing to the park:

Parent: "Now I'll write down what you say. Shall we call this story *Riverside Park?*" (Selecting a title can help your child focus on what she is writing about. It is not an essential step if your child is eager to talk. Or, a title can be chosen after the story is complete.)

Child: "Yes!"

Parent: (Write the title *Riverside Park*, and print beneath it, *by Nicole Robins*. Read aloud what you have written so far.) "Now what would you like to say?"

Child: "I went on the slide. It was sort of scary."

Parent: (Print "*I went on the slide. It was sort of scary*," reading each word to your child as you print it.) "Is there anything else you'd like to say?"

Child: "Yea. I saw Jesse."

Parent: (Print "*I saw Jesse.*" Repeat each word aloud as you write.)

Reread all sentences and ask for any additions. You may ask questions to encourage your child to say more, but respect her judgment when she says her story is finished. The tale needn't be long or elaborate. The above example would make a fine first story. Soon you'll find that if you extend her language with discussion *before* you start writing, colorful stories will result.

When the story is finished, read it with much expression and enthusiasm as you point to each word. Read the title and author's name with pride. Now invite your child to read along with you as you point to each word. If you've accurately recorded her exact words, she may be able to read much of it herself. She'll probably enjoy illustrating her story. You may wish to date the stories and save them in a binder. Vary this activity from time to time, by using a computer or typewriter to record your child's words.

THE CONVENTIONS OF WRITING

There's much to learn about the conventions of writing: letters are formed in a specific direction; there are spaces between words; words must flow from left to right; lines of print are horizontal and proceed from the top of the page to the bottom. These conventions will not be followed in initial writing attempts. Through repeated experimentation and exposure to good models (your writing and books), however, writing conventions will begin to appear in your child's work.

Children intuitively request writing models when they ask you to label their drawings or write important phrases for them. Make the most of these precious, teachable moments. As you write out the requested word, say and exaggerate each letter sound, orally blending the sounds together. You provide an immediate model for how writing works. You can write words on scrap paper for your child to copy onto her work. Or, write the word using a yellow felt marker and invite her to write with pencil or pen over your lines. Typical requests are: *To: Dad; To: Mom; From: Jessica; I love you.* You'll find your child drilling herself on these phrases by copying them again and again, modeling your writing, and soon writing on her own. They'll appear on pictures and messages to you. Handwriting and writing conventions are practiced naturally when her goal is communication.

When your child starts to form letters, encourage a conventional pencil hold. Use of a standard, soft-lead pencil promotes a correct, relaxed hold. A "child's pencil" is too fat for comfortable writing. Place the pencil in proper position in the hand she usually uses to draw. The pencil should be held between the thumb and index finger about an inch above the pencil point. The index finger will be on top and the pencil will rest comfortably on or near the first joint of the middle finger. If your child is happy writing with a plastic pencil grip, try using one for correct finger placement.

Never indicate that your child has written something incorrectly. Fluency in writing and the easy flow of ideas must come before the use of writing conventions, or your child will not see the purpose of what to her are arbitrary rules. The joy and flow of writing are paramount!

PHONICS IN PERSPECTIVE

When spelling becomes essential to your child for communicating her ideas, it's the ideal time to introduce phonics. Phonics is the relationship between letter symbols and speech sounds. In actuality, those letter symbols are a code. Phonics is the tool for cracking that code in order to derive meaning, or using the code to build new words.

When a reader encounters an unknown word, phonics gives an approximation of its sound. She takes this information, along with meaning and structure clues from the passage, and searches her memory for the right word. Look what the reader does in this case: "The kitten drank some *milk*." She combines knowledge of letter sounds ("m-m-m") with knowledge of kittens ("I remember those kittens at Jake's house drinking milk like crazy.") and makes a sensible guess: "The kitten drank some m-m-milk."

Phonics acts as a conduit for bringing language to print. It gives children control over their learning because it allows them to independently decipher the many new words they encounter. It's also vital for putting letters together to form words when writing. Indeed, studies confirm that children who receive phonics instruction emerge as stronger readers. Marilyn Adams evaluated the vast body of research on reading instruction in her authoritative work, *Learning to Read*, and arrived at this conclusion: "Approaches in which systematic code instruction is included along with the reading of meaningful connected text result in superior reading achievement overall."

Learning phonics is an abstract exercise without first having experienced the need for this skill. As we've seen, meaning must be the driving force behind learning to read and write. Children will show an interest in sound-letter correspondence when they realize it's the key for figuring out the unknown words they wish to read and for putting their own important ideas into print. So phonics instruction begins in response to a child's desire to communicate and not as an isolated skill. Instruction should be just enough to start her down the road to reading and writing, allowing her to put ideas into print and decode words new to her reading vocabulary. Learning language sounds, the letters that represent them, and how those letters grow into words achieves this goal.

HOW TO BEGIN

The sound-symbol relationships of phonics should be learned in the same spirit that your child learns how a seed grows into a tree or how the toaster works. When your child shows interest in how letters grow into words and how "words work," show her. The following instructions do not represent lessons. Instead, these are the pieces of information needed to be able to create words. Explanation is best kept short and examples given over a period of time. You may end up talking about language sounds in the car, sounding out words while differentiating her choice in breakfast cereal from the other brands, or blending -at words on a napkin while your child munches her lunch.

Let your child learn about phonics at her own rate. There are many discoveries to make that could take several months or more than a year. Your child needs a lot of time to explore the many sounds, and the letter symbols that represent those sounds. Present one sound, letter, or word family at a time. Go back and review frequently. If you notice any frustration, return to more comfortable ground. Don't feel you must teach every aspect of phonics described below. Any amount of exposure to the concept that sounds can be represented by symbols goes a long way to strengthening beginning reading and writing ability.

LEARNING LANGUAGE SOUNDS

The key to understanding phonics is an awareness of the sound units of speech, called phonemes, and how to represent them with letters. Children rightfully focus on the meaning of words and not the phonemes that compose words. To prepare your child for spelling and figuring out unknown words as she reads, you'll first need to develop an awareness of pho-nemes. The cooing baby ("b-b-b-b"), the roaring toddler ("R-R-R-R-o-a-r-r-r-r!"), and the chanting child ("Blip-blop, poola-poola") are already expert at making the fascinating sounds of language. The next step is playful exploration of how sound units come together to form words.

At this point you are only talking about sounds — not printed letters — so these activities can even take place in the car. The easiest sound to hear is the one that begins a word. Pick a sound, then create experiences with words that begin with that sound. If your child's name is Beth, than

/b/ is the phoneme to start with (/b/ refers to the phoneme or language sound that starts *bed* and *b* refers to the letter name, *bee*). Blowing *b*ubbles, baking *b*read, and bathing *b*abies are perfect activities to share and talk about while your child learns about /b/. Talk about the similar beginning sound of these /b/ words. Ask her to think of other words beginning with the same sound. What better time to learn /b/ than while enjoying a ripe /b/anana! Continue adding new sounds to your child's repertoire by talking about the sounds that start different special words.

After your child can easily identify the phonemes that start many words, draw her attention to the phonemes that end words. Exploring families of rhyming words helps your child hear these end sounds. Take turns creating the longest possible list of rhyming words: *cat, bat, hat, mat, rat,* or *tall, small, fall, ball, hall,* and so on.

LEARNING LETTERS

To learn sight vocabulary, your child associates a printed word with the spoken word it represents. Now she'll learn to associate a printed letter symbol with the sound it represents. Therefore, it's important to focus on letter sounds and not letter names. Calling out the letter names "see-a-tee" won't decipher or spell the word cat. Blending the individual sounds /c/-/a/-/t/ will. Letter names are easily learned from children's educational television shows and the *ABC Song*. Although this song teaches letter names and alphabetical order, it does not help children sound out words.

For an example of how to start, let's introduce the printed letter b and the sound it represents. Start by showing your child the letter. You may print it on blank paper or on a marker board. You may find it written in a book or on a sign. It may begin one of her special words, or you may use the *b Letter-Sound Card* in Activity Materials on page 167. Enthusiastically say, "This letter makes the sound, /b/" while pointing to the letter. (Remember to make the sound of /b/ as in *bed*. Do not say *bee*.) Have her repeat the sound while looking at the letter.

This manuscript style allows most letters to be formed easily with one continuous slant stroke. The transition to cursive writing is natural, yet the print is similar to book print. You may wish to contact the school your child will be attending for a copy of the alphabet used in their writing program.

While she's learning to make the /b/ sound upon seeing *b*, teach her to write *b*. Write several *b*'s on a blank sheet of paper as you make the /b/ sound. Be sure to use the correct directional movement (see manuscript chart, page 82). Now print a few b's with a yellow marker pen. Let her write on top of your lines. Next, let her print her version beneath your model. If she needs help, gently hold her hand as you print the letter together.

Tracing with a pencil directly over numerous letter examples is tedious work and discourages children from writing. It's better to let your child practice letters on her own again and again among scribbles and drawings. Encourage her to use the letter in her pretend writing when she wants to communicate a word beginning with /b/.

Continue by teaching the following letters. They are good to introduce because of their frequency of use in writing, their distinctive appearance and sound, and their versatility to form many words: *a, c, f, n, p, r, s, t*. For now, present only the hard sound of /c/ as in *cat* (not *city*). Also, teach the short vowel sounds such as /a/ as in *apple* (not *ate*). Short vowels are used more frequently and they are necessary for learning the short vowel word groups below. Long vowel sounds are simply the letter names and are easily learned at the same time your child learns all letter names

BLENDING SOUNDS TO PRODUCE WORDS

Don't wait until your child knows every letter before you empower her with the ability to blend letter sounds together to produce words. You can present this skill after she learns just the eight sounds above. Knowing the principle of rhyme and a word's first letter sound will enable her to sound out and spell words from the same word family. Once she can sound out *can*, it's easy to sound out *fan, pan, ran*, and *tan*. Read aloud the word family lists below so she gets a feel for the similar sound within each word family. Then take turns rhyming words with *bat, can*, and *cap*.

In the following activity, let her watch you write so she can sense how words are constructed in left-right sequence. Help her track by pointing to each letter as she reads.

1. Print *cat* on blank paper. Pointing to each letter, help her sound and blend together /c/-/a/-/t/ to make *cat*. Share her joy in finding meaning in a group of letters!

2. Next, print *f* in front of *at* to make *fat*. Help her sound out *fat* just as you did *cat*.

3. Now let your child spell *cat* and *fat*. If she's able to write letters, slowly sound out the words as she repeats and writes each word. Or she can arrange the letters in *Word Construction* to create words (see Activities, page 92).

> **/a/ as in *apple***
> -at: cat, fat, pat, rat, sat
> -an: can, fan, pan, ran, tan
> -ap: cap, nap, tap

Continue teaching the remaining *at, an*, and *ap* words. Reinforce her awareness that she's reading and spelling real words. Now, write these short vowel words on cards and use them along with her special words in chapter 5 Activities, such as *Word Link-Up*.

LEARNING MORE LETTERS AND BLENDED WORDS

Now that your child understands that letters represent language sounds and she's applied the skill to actual reading and spelling, she's probably eager to learn more sounds. Continue with those that begin her special sight words: for example *h* from *hug* or *m* from *mud.* Help your child combine word identification skills (sight words and phonics) by emphasizing the first letter of each special word you present with your voice and pointing finger. Present capital letters if words begin with them: for example *T* from *Tanya* or *B* from *Big Bird.* Continue helping your child sound out environmental print. Be sure to offer those letter sounds she needs to communicate her ideas in writing.

Introduce rhyming word families for the rest of the short vowels.

/e/ as in *egg*
-en: Ben, den, hen, Jen, Ken, Len, men, pen, ten,
-et: bet, get, jet, let, met, net, pet, set, vet, wet
-ed: bed, fed, Jed, led, Ned, red, Ted, wed

/i/ as in *igloo*
-in: bin, din, fin, kin, pin, sin, tin, win
-it: bit, fit, hit, kit, lit, mitt, pit, sit, wit
-ig: big, dig, fig, jig, pig, rig, wig

/o/ as in *octopus*
-op: flop, hop, mop, pop, stop, top
-ock: dock, flock, lock, mock, rock, sock
-ot: dot, got, hot, jot, lot, not, pot, tot

/u/ as in *umbrella*
-un: bun, fun, gun, nun, pun, run, sun
-up: cup, pup, sup
-ut: but, cut, gut, hut, jut, mutt, nut, rut,

Note that some of the words begin with blends such as *st-* or *fl-* or end with doubled letters such as *-tt.* Treat formation of these words no differently than the others. Simply run your finger beneath the word, blending all of the sounds within that word together. After your child is comfortable with short word families, introduce silent *e* as a way to change the sound of the vowel from short to long. Play a game where "powerful silent *e*" can make these changes: hop-hope, fin-fine, rob-robe, cut-cute, cub-cube. Introduce long vowel words in families such as these: -ake, -ame, -ine, -ice, -one.

There are many phonics rules a child could learn. But with so many rules and exceptions to them, children are better off spending their time engaged in actual reading and writing than in memorizing rules. Understanding the concept of blending letter sounds together to form words, combined with meaning and structure clues, will help your child spell and identify most of the words she writes and encounters in reading (see *Phonics in Perspective,* this chapter). Just as your child intuitively deduces grammar rules from being immersed in oral language, she'll similarly deduce phonics rules, on her own, as her experiences with written language grow. Remember: Reading is discovering meaning in print. Writing is putting meaning into print. Phonics is a means to those ends, not an end in itself.

INVENTED SPELLING

Knowledge of letter sounds and formation will merge with your child's interest in recording her ideas. What better way to practice phonics than to put it to use. If your child is attempting to sound out words as she writes, help her hear the individual sounds within the word by making and exaggerating those sounds as you write. If she is able, let her figure out what letters she needs to write as she sounds out the word. If she is unsure of how to form a letter, show her on a separate sheet of paper. Provide her with a model alphabet for reference (see page 82). The on-the-spot phonics lesson you offer as parent/consultant is the most effective way your child will ever learn this skill. Phonics is learned as an integral part of her quest to convey an important message.

Remember that, at first, the beginning letter sound represents an entire word to children. Next, they become aware of the end sound so that *hs* represents *house*. Later, come consonants and vowels in the middle of the word. If she invents spellings such as *krfl* for *careful*, she's doing an excellent job of communicating and applying her rudimentary knowledge of phonics. Children who are encouraged to use invented spellings won't shy away from using rich vocabulary in their writing. For them, *enrms* (enormous) is just as easy to spell as *big*. Any author will tell you, it's a far greater challenge to get ideas flowing than to spell words correctly.

If your child's invented spellings are logical and show an understanding for the letter sounds she has learned thus far, treat them as the wonderful achievements they are. Spelling becomes more conventional as children gain more experience with words. Communication is the goal of writing, so applaud your child's early efforts.

Invented spelling puts children firmly in control of their own writing. It empowers them with the ability to communicate their own ideas without being dependent on anyone else.

WRITING FOR AN AUDIENCE

The purpose of writing is to communicate. Unless there is an audience for one's work, it's not fun or meaningful to produce. Here are formats for making your child's writing "public":

 GREETING CARDS

Saying *Happy Birthday, Thank You,* or *Get Well* with an original greeting card provides excellent first writing experience by combining short written messages with drawings.

 WRITING SCRAPBOOK

Save her writing in a binder. Your child will take pride in rereading her work. Over time you'll both enjoy a tremendous sense of achievement as you watch your child's writing ability unfold.

 LETTER WRITING

Nothing could be more rewarding for a budding writer than a reply to her letter. The process validates writing as an important communication skill.

 ENVIRONMENTAL PRINT

Encourage your child to create functional signs for your home: *Jason's Room, Quiet, No Pets Here,* or place cards for dinner time. Post-it-Notes™ in the 3" x 5" size work great.

 BEST-SELLERS

In the next chapter, you'll see how to turn your child's written language into books.

Be sure to welcome all forms of writing: scribbles, pictures, letter shapes, letters, pretend writing, and conventional writing.

LEARNING TO WRITE BY WRITING

Remember, as with any language skill, learning to write is a slow, but sure process. Children learn best by doing: They learn speech by speaking and they learn literacy by actually reading and writing. So provide rich, written language models and ample opportunities for your child to freely explore and use written language. Children become able and enthusiastic writers when they experience writing, firsthand, as a powerful tool for communicating *their* important ideas.

WRITING

WARMING-UP

Mastering the following skills is not a prerequisite to learning to read or write. They will, however, strengthen the eye-hand coordination and fine muscle control needed for writing. Remember, add language by talking about these activities and you'll be improving reading comprehension and writing ability.

 DRESSING

Let her zip, button, lace, and snap her own clothing.

 SEWING

Let her sew with a large plastic needle and yarn. She can stitch loosely woven cloth held tightly in an embroidery hoop. Let her stitch through the lattice of a plastic strawberry basket.

 DRAWING

Encourage free-style drawing with pencils, pens, markers, crayons, and chalk.

 TRACING

Let her trace around the edge of a cookie cutter, jar lid, ruler — or even her hand or foot. She may like to color in her tracing. Following a maze will help her draw along a set path and predict where she'll end up.

 TRANSFERRING

Let her transfer beans, popcorn, or cotton balls with tongs, tweezers, or a spoon from a full bowl on the left to an empty bowl on the right. Colored water can be transferred from a bowl to sections of an ice cube tray using an eye dropper.

CUTTING

Offer a pair of children's scissors that cut easily without causing frustration. Try the plastic kind with metal blades. First let your child cut paper freely. Then let her cut along lines and shapes she's drawn. She may want to paste her shapes on colored paper.

 FOLDING

She can make a fan by chanting, following, and repeating these instructions, "Fold-press-flip." With a sheet of paper, she makes a narrow fold, then presses it firmly. Next she flips the paper to the other side and repeats the instructions. She'll eventually end up with an accordion-fold fan.

 STRINGING

Your child can string beads, buttons, Cheerios™, macaroni, or cut-up straws. Thread a large plastic needle with yarn, or tightly tape one end of a piece of yarn or string to make it stiff. Narrow plastic tubing works well with large wooden beads.

WRITING DEVICES

Let your child create words by "pecking away" on a typewriter or computer. Any adult word-processing program is fine. Just set the font size to about 18 points. It's also fun to use punch-out label makers, rubber stamp alphabets, or magnetic letters.

SENTENCE PUZZLE

Have your child write out a sentence on a long strip of paper. Now have her snip each word apart. Mix up the words. Can she put the sentence back in order by repeating her sentence as she hunts for the needed words? She may enjoy taping the words together to form the original sentence or she may prefer to leave the words separated and try to put it together another time. She can explore other ways the words will form sentences and add new words.

VIVID LETTERS

Make learning to write a rich experience involving all five senses. Have your child make the sound of each letter as she writes.

• Be adventurous! Let your child create letters with toothpaste, shaving cream, whipped cream, or fingerpaint. She can write on a foggy window, or in sand at the beach.

• Fill a tray with sand or cornmeal. Have her form letters and words by writing on the tray with her finger.

• Write letters on stiff cardboard. Let your child trace them with glue and then sprinkle sand or grain on them. Now she has a set of textured letters to feel.

• Give her a paintbrush and water to write on an outdoor wall or concrete.

• Encourage her to write using paint, crayons, or chalk.

• Write letters, words, or messages to each other on a chalk or marker board.

• Let her "write" letters on a wall at night with a flashlight.

• While on the go, have your child use her index finger like a pencil to write letters in the air. Or, form letters with your fingers on each other's hands. Can you feel what the letter is?

• Help your child make letters from clay, or, for even more fun, cookie dough. Bake and eat your letter cookies!

OFFICE

Create a business-like office stocked with stationery, envelopes, Post-it-Notes™, paper clips, stapler, pads of paper, office signs (*Open, Closed, Will Return, No Smoking, Jessica Hamilton, President*), receipt books, rubber stamps (including one with her name), erasers, pens, pencils, markers — whatever she needs to be an efficient writer. Make or purchase desk organizers. Even start a filing system in a cardboard box or drawer for your child's writing. Let your child make business cards for herself by cutting up and writing on index cards. Go to your local office supply store together to find "real stuff." Add business forms such as those provided for *Real World Reading*, Activities, chapter 3.

MULTI-MEDIA MASTERPIECES

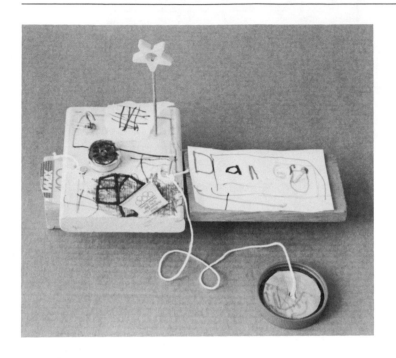

Children from literacy-rich homes seem to naturally create collages and "junk sculpture." They'll cut, paste, staple, and tie a variety of materials together to make pretend or free-form objects. They'll also add writing to their creations. Set aside a box of magazines, lightweight cardboard cereal boxes, tape, string, marking pens, and other castoffs that may strike your child's imagination. Encourage your child to engage in this very imaginative form of construction play that takes print beyond the confines of paper.

I CAN WRITE MY NAME

Your child's first written word should be the one that's most meaningful to her: her name. She'll learn these letters faster than any others. Create a permanent model for her by printing her name on a card. Have blank paper on hand so she can practice copying your model whenever she's interested. As with all writing, learning to write your name is most interesting and meaningful in functional contexts. Here are some ideas:

- Signing her artistic masterpieces

- Signing greeting cards

- Creating a place card for herself at mealtime

- Creating badges for pretend play.

PORTABLE OFFICE

Keep a portable office in your purse and make waiting time fun and productive. Use a zippered pencil case to hold a small pad, ballpoint pen, a few colored pencils, a pair of scissors, and a glue stick. Now your child is ready to write anytime, anywhere.

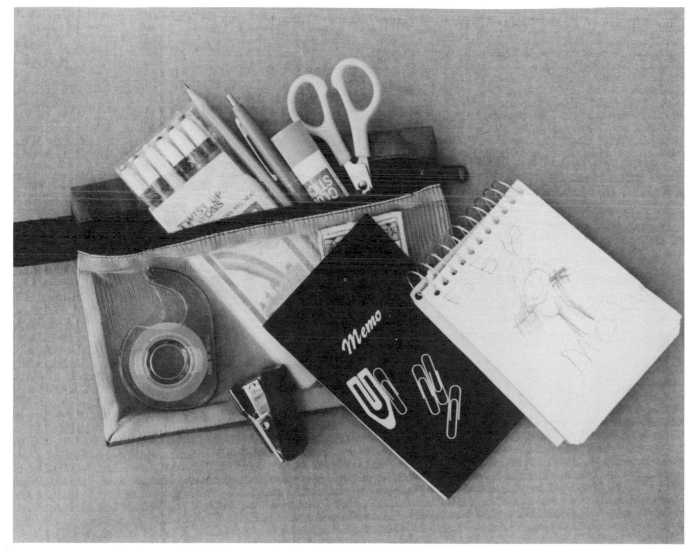

PHONICS FUN

LETTER-SOUND CARDS

Use these cards to teach the letter sounds and play *Match, Recall,* and *Pairs* (see *Special Word Cards,* Activities, on page 70). This time, match the letter to the picture that begins with the same letter sound. For example, match *a* with the apple picture. Remember, always start with only two or three match choices, gradually increasing to include all nine.

 SOUNDS-AROUND

Have fun using cards to label household objects with their first letters. Take turns matching each other's body parts and clothing with their first letters.

 OBJECT-SOUND SORT

Let your child sort a variety of objects by the letter sound that begins their names, beneath appropriate *Letter-Sound Cards.* Begin with two letter sounds to choose from. Add more as she progresses.

WORD CONSTRUCTION

These letter cards provide a very effective hands-on activity for discovering letter-sound relationships and patterns within words. Let your child arrange these letters to spell familiar and new words. (See Activity Materials, page 174.)

 MAKE-A-WORD

Place just a few letters and word parts before her. Now say a word slowly, clearly enunciating each letter sound as she repeats the word and selects the correct letters, "/p/-/a/-/n/, pan." Try sounding out nonsense or "robot talk" words that follow the same short vowel pattern: *nan, san, tat, nab.*

 PICK-A-PART

Place the individual consonant letter cards into one bowl. Put the word segment cards (*an, ap, at*) into another bowl. Take turns drawing one card from each bowl. If you can make a real word with your cards, keep it. If you can't, return them. Cooperate to make as many real words as you both can.

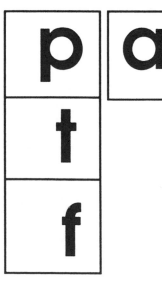

NAME IT!

Gather a few items for your child to name, such as a cup, apple, toy car, or block. Let her name each item by arranging letters beneath it. Remember to welcome invented spelling such as *cp* or *apl*.

MAGICIAN

Form *cat*. Now say, "Abracadabra, I'll change the *cat* into a *bat*." Change only the first letter. Now let her be the magician and change *bat* into *rat, sat*, or *fat*.

DICTIONARY SCRAPBOOK

Print letters your child knows in the corner of each page of heavy paper. She can find magazine pictures to go with each letter and paste them on that page, or draw her own pictures. Label each picture with its name. Keep the pages in a three-ring binder so more pages can be added and placed in alphabetical order as more letters are learned. She can also create more imaginative alphabet books following the examples of Van Allsburg's *The Z Was Zapped*, Base's *Animalia*, or Kitamura's *What's Inside*.

RHYMING

RHYMING OBJECTS

Collect pairs of objects and/or magazine photographs of objects with names that rhyme: bug, mug; car, jar; fork, cork. Let your child name each object as she places it next to its rhyming partner.

MISSING WORD

Read familiar nursery rhymes, songs, stories, or poems (Dr. Seuss is ideal). Leave out the rhyming word and let your child predict it: "I do not like them, Sam-I-Am. I do not like green eggs and . . . ." This game can be played on the go by reciting the rhymes.

I'M AN ARTIST

On blank paper, write one of your child's silly rhyming sentences for her to illustrate: *A fat cat sat on a rat.*

DR. SEUSS

Dr. Seuss was a genius for creating imaginative, relevant reading material that develops phonics skills. His books offer beginning readers a perfect blend of poetry, phonics, and fun. Offer your child books from his *Beginner Books* reading series. All of his books make great read-alouds.

 SPY-A-SOUND

Pick a favorite letter sound, then take turns finding things in the environment that start with that sound.

 WORD TALK

Simply talk about how words are constructed. Say a simple word and analyze the different sounds you hear within that word. Start by identifying sounds that begin the word. When your child is adept at this, help her to identify end sounds and later, middle sounds.

 FIND-A-RHYME

Think of something that could be found in a kitchen, a toy box, or elsewhere, and give a clue that rhymes with its name. "I'm thinking of something you can see outside the car window. It rhymes with *ball*." "Oh, I see the *mall*."

 I'M A POET

Create a poem together. Take turns saying the first line or rhyming the second line.

 PHONEME SONG

To the tune of *The Farmer in the Dell*, sing, "Zebra starts with /z/. Zipper starts with /z/. Hi, ho, the dairy-o. Zoo starts with /z/." Or, simplify the song by repeating only one word throughout the verse. Now pick a new letter, "Turtle starts with /t/. . ." Remember to sing the phoneme sound and not the letter name.

 SOUND CATEGORIES

Adapt the category games in chapter 2 for phonics practice. Let letter sounds become the category. For example, the choices for *Odd Man Out* might be, *pot, hot, ran, dot*. Or for *Brainstorm*, think of words that start like *monkey*. *Classify It* can be played with /s/ words or /n/ words. Which category for *nut, sandwich*, or *sad*?

CHAPTER 7

Creating Books

I AM AN AUTHOR

THE POWER OF WRITTEN LANGUAGE

There's no better way for children to experience the power of written language than to create their own books. If you've read aloud to your child and filled your home with books, he already values them as very special possessions. Creating books tells your child that his words are important. Creating books also strongly establishes the self-concept that he is an author, fully able to share his knowledge through written language.

WHAT IS A BOOK?

You may think of a book as a beautifully bound masterpiece selling thousands of copies each year. But to a child, a few sheets of paper stapled along one edge and filled with his own writing and drawings are a masterpiece. The dictionary defines *book* as, "a volume made of pages fastened along one edge enclosed between a protective cover." It's this simple definition that allows children to become instant authors and publishers.

GETTING STARTED

Don't wait until your child is an experienced writer before suggesting he write a book. When presented with a booklet of blank pages, most children are eager to jump right in and write. Even a child at the "scribble" stage can participate. Fold a sheet of paper in half, and cut along the fold. Put two half sheets together and fold them in half again. Staple them down the center. Present this inspiring little booklet to your child and let him create a book by writing and/or drawing on the pages.

As soon as your child can handle a pair of scissors, a pencil, and a stapler, he's ready to create books on his own. Supply him with this equipment and some paper. After many experiences with books, he will have a concept of what one should look like. Have one available to serve as a model. Or, he may prefer to freely make the book in his own way. He can cut the pages to the desired size, and staple the left edge. He can decorate the cover, and write and draw whatever he likes on the inside pages. Invite him to read his book to you. Marvel at the success of his project.

Older children may prefer to copy a story they have already written onto unbound pages, and then assemble the book. This gives them more flexibility to add, revise, or eliminate material as they work.

FIRST READING BOOKS

Make photocopies of the books provided in Activity Materials on pages 143, 156, 165, 177, 179, and 181. Cut pages out along the dotted lines. Fold along the solid lines. Put the pages in order. Staple through the center or along the folded edge.

First Reading Books serve as models for book-making. Their structure familiarizes your child with book format and assures success. The sentence springboards on each page give him something familiar to write about, while inviting him to fill in the blanks with his own ideas and words.

At first you may want to write the words your child dictates. Later, he'll write on his own. *About the book* gives him a sense of what the book will be about. *About the author* gives him a chance to shine. Your child can illustrate the pages as suggested in *Illustrations* on page 101. Encourage friends and family to enter comments in the review section on the back cover. The books lend themselves to creating spin-offs. Use each book as a model for more writing and reading fun. Here are some variations:

- **I Love:** Mommy Loves, Jason Loves, Grandma Loves
- **— Can:** Elephants Can, Babies Can, Fish Can
- **I Eat!:** I Eat, with each page stating your child's favorite food.
- **Hello:** A book from the point of view of the morning sun, the night moon, or an animal.

THE POSSIBILITIES ARE ENDLESS

First Reading Books are just a start. What follows are a wealth of book-making options for creating anything from the simple to the sublime; from the spontaneous to the planned. Don't be overwhelmed. It's better to encourage your child to create many books than to tire him out on one elaborate project. Pick and chose those ideas most interesting to your child. Use these ideas as a way to maintain interest when you hear, "I don't know what to write about" or "What other kind of book can I make?"

An idea for a book can come from any-where. These ideas will spark your child's creativity and encourage imaginative stories and books. Let him write or dictate about:

 EXPERIENCES

Invite your child to write about his world.

- Topics on which he's an expert: *My Toys, A Trip to the Store,* or *Noisy Sounds*
- Activities you've shared
- Daily field trips
- Discoveries of how things feel, sound, look, taste, or smell
- Dreams and nightmares
- Holidays.

 ART

Invite your child to describe a picture or write a story inspired by a picture. Here are some art sources:

- Newspaper or magazine images
- Family photographs
- Famous paintings
- An imaginary creature he's drawn
- Any original drawing.

 IF'S

Enter a world of fantasy and imagination with an *If* story.

- If I could fly . . .
- If I shrunk . . .
- If I were a giant . . .
- If it snowed marshmallows . . .
- If I were Mom and she were I . . .
- If I were a telephone (on any object, animal, person) . . .

MUSIC

Let music be the inspiration.

- Variations. After creating your own variation of a favorite song, make it into a songbook. For example, your child could create a book entitled *The Storm* as a take-off on the song, *The Wheels on the Bus.* "... The rain from the sky goes plop, plop, plop, all through the town" (see chapter 3).
- Recordings. Play a favorite piece of music, not necessarily a child's song, such as a classical, jazz, or folk recording. Invite your child to describe the piece or write a story inspired by the music.

 FAVORITE STORIES

Favorite books can inspire writing.

- Spin-offs. Your child can create his own versions. Those you've read aloud provide models to help structure his own ideas. For example, instead of *If You Give a Mouse a Cookie*, your child might write, *If You Give a Monster Some Bubble Gum*. Or, his version of *Goodnight, Moon* might be called *Good Morning, Sun* and be about himself saying good morning to all the special objects in his own room. These books also lend themselves to spin-off versions.
- A list of wishes from *Someday*
- A collection of sounds, smells, or tastes from *Crash! Bang! Boom!*
- An account of life with a peacock's tail from *Imogene's Antlers*
- A story of fortunate and unfortunate events from *Fortunately*
- An account of an animal or creature's walk from *Rosie's Walk*
- A tale of those weird red or blue things from *Those Green Things*.

 SENTENCE SPRINGBOARDS

Start with those your child is familiar with from *First Reading Books*. With springboards he can inventory likes, dislikes, abilities, ... anything.
- I love . . .
- I can . . . But, I can't . . .
- Spiders can . . . But, spiders can't . . .
- I wish . . .
- I'll never . . .
- I'd like to . . .
- I'm happy when . . .
- I'm angry when . . .
- I love to . . . because . . .
- I hate to . . . because . . .
- When I was little, I . . .
- When I grow up, I'll . . .

 SEQUELS

What adventures are in store for the Billy Goats Gruff on the other side of the bridge? Will Baby Bear visit Goldilocks? Is Cinderella really suited for castle life? Might other creatures threaten the Three Little Pigs?

 POINTS OF VIEW

Tell a tale from the point of view of the Big Bad Wolf, the Troll, or the Wicked Witch.

KINDS OF BOOKS

Look through your home or community library for examples of these and other genres and formats. Then, encourage your child to create his own versions.

 AUTOBIOGRAPHY OR BIOGRAPHY

Write about himself, a friend, or a relative.

 HOW-TO

Let your child describe steps for building with Legos™, making a sandwich, playing a game, or any other activity on which he's an expert.

 ALPHABET BOOK OR DICTIONARY

Books can list words related to a particular subject such as, *The Animal ABC's*, or *Dictionary of Toys*.

 COMIC BOOK

Your child can make a comic story with original characters and dialogue balloons. Comic books are fun to make for those who love to draw. For those who don't, cut and paste small pieces of paper over the dialogue balloons of a favorite comic strip. Cut apart the boxes and paste one on each page of the book.

 WORDLESS BOOK

Here's another favorite for illustrators. The challenge is to make each picture detailed and informative enough to tell the story.

FACT BOOK

Your child can share his expertise on rocks, pets, swimming, or other topics.

 TRAVEL GUIDE

He can write a guide to his own town or a city he has visited.

 SHAPE BOOKS

Help your child cut pages and covers in a particular shape. A triangular book can display triangular-shaped objects. Fold and cut paper into sixteenths for a tiny book. Use strips of paper to make a book of long, thin things. An animal-shaped book can give facts about that animal.

PARTS OF A BOOK

Children take great pride in making their books look "real." Help your child accomplish this by looking at and analyzing favorite books together. How are they similar? What type of pages do most books include? Do nonfiction books have a different format than fiction? Now invite your child to add some of the book parts you've discovered together. He may choose to include any or all of these elements to make his books look "real."

 FRONT COVER

People do judge a book by its cover. Your child should make the book irresistible by designing a catchy cover. Be sure the title and author are prominent. Include inviting illustrations showing what the book is about. The cover can be made from heavier stock than the pages, such as construction paper or cardboard.

 INSIDE FRONT COVER

This is the place to tell about the book. The story or topic is summarized. Perhaps a passage is quoted.

TITLE PAGE

The title, author, and illustrator are given. The publishing company and its location are often included.

 COPYRIGHT PAGE

The copyright date and information are given. Use the copyright as a fun way to date your child's precious creation.

 DEDICATION PAGE

This page lets the author show appreciation for a special person or persons who have influenced his life or his book. "This book is dedicated to my mom because she reads me a book every night."

 ACKNOWLEDGEMENT PAGE

The author lists those people or groups who helped with the book project.
Note: Title, copyright, dedication, and acknowledgement pages may be combined into one or two pages.

 TABLE OF CONTENTS

This page is needed when a book has several chapters. Chapter titles are listed, followed by the page number on which they start.

 BODY

This is the most important section. These are the pages on which the story or information is written and illustrated.

 INSIDE BACK COVER

Information is generally given about the author. Who is he? How old is he and where does he live? What are his hobbies? Has he written other books?

 BACK COVER

Here is the publisher's last chance to sell the book to the prospective reader. Give a sales pitch about why your book is wonderful. Your child can include those great book reviews received from important people who have read his book.

ILLUSTRATIONS

Your child may want to illustrate his book after he's written a sentence or two on each page, or he can start with illustrations, then describe them. Also, he may prefer to paste pre-drawn illustrations on the pages rather than draw directly on them. This gives him flexibility to re-draw if he does not like his first attempt. Here are various illustration options:

 ORIGINAL ART

He can use marking pens, colored pencils, crayons, or paste in pre-drawn pictures.

 PHOTOGRAPHS

Your child will enjoy posing for photographs when he knows his picture will appear in a book. For example, he can pose with favorite foods and toys to illustrate *I Love*. He'll pride himself in demonstrating jumping, flying, or running for *I Can*. Discarded photos of family, friends, and pets can find a place in *Hi*.

 MAGAZINE PHOTOS

He can create a collage by pasting parts of different photos on the same page.

 FLAT ITEMS

A book about leaves or flowers could have actual pressed leaves or flowers taped or glued to the pages.

BINDING

To be a book, paper must be ". . . fastened along one edge." Here are some binding options.

 STAPLED

This is the fastest, easiest way. The big advantage to stapling is that even the youngest book producer can take charge of the binding process.

 PLASTIC STRIPS

These slide along the edge of clear plastic covers. They are available in stationery departments. Help your child cut them to the desired length.

 COMB-BOUND

Bring his creation to a quick-print shop with a comb-binding machine.

 REPORT FOLDERS OR BINDERS

These work well for 8 1/2" by 11" sheets. Binders can hold collections of writing and drawings done over time, because you can open them to add or reorganize materials.

 RINGS OR YARN

Reinforce the holes by first taping the spots to be punched. Now punch the holes. Then put rings or yarn through
the holes to hold the pages together.

 STITCHED

Using heavy thread, a sturdy needle, and a thimble, you can easily stitch through four

GENERATING AN AUDIENCE

Books are written to be read! Writing thrives when there's an appreciative audience for your child's work. Here are ways to give his books the audience they deserve.

 READ THEM ALOUD

Your child can be an audience for his own books. Read them along with the trade books you read aloud. He can read books aloud to friends, relatives, even stuffed toys.

 EXHIBIT THEM

Make your child's books part of your home library. Leave them out among the reading material on your coffee table.

 GIVE THEM AS GIFTS OR DONATIONS

Original books make precious gifts — especially for grandparents. Share books at school or the library.

 PRINT COPIES

You can make several copies of your child's book using a copying machine. This gives him the experience of having a book "in print" and makes it easier to part with it. Older writers may enjoy selling their books lemonade stand-style.

PARENT-MADE BOOKS

Parent-made books make ideal first reading materials. You can tailor the books you make to your child's interests and use the special words he is able to read.

 FIRST READING BOOKS

Make a set of *First Reading Books* and their variations, showcasing your child's special words.

 MORE STRUCTURES FOR SPECIAL WORDS

Create more contexts in which your child can read his special words by using sentence springboards. (See *What's the Big Idea?* on page 98). Or try this structure: *Play, Nicole, play. Go, Mommy, go. Jump, Daddy, jump. Jump, kangaroo, jump.* Mix different names with different actions.

 LANGUAGE EXPERIENCE STORIES

Keep the stories your child dictates to you in a binder labeled with his name. Date the entries. Let him illustrate the pages. Or, rewrite his favorite language-experience stories onto bound pages.

 JUST WHAT HE SAID

You may hear your child spontaneously singing an original song in the bathtub, telling himself an amusing story while engrossed in play, or uttering a profound statement to his dog. Take note! Record his words and save them to create a book at a more convenient time. He'll be amazed to see his words transformed into a book.

Also listen for words your child repeats again and again. Use these as a refrain throughout a predictable book: *Never, My turn, No way*, or *For sure*. Just keep your ears open to create very personal books.

 PHOTO ALBUM BOOKS

A photo album becomes a sturdy reading book when photographs or illustrations and text are slipped between its plastic pages.

PERSONALIZED COMMERCIAL BOOKS

Tailor inexpensive variety store books or illustrated calendars to your child's beginning reading needs. Paste blank paper over the text or dates, and replace them with words your child can read. He now has a personalized, professionally illustrated book.

 BOARD BOOKS

Ring together pre-punched large-size index cards to make original, changeable board books.

 MY CHILD, THE HERO

Write a story starring none other than your favorite kid.

READING ORIGINAL BOOKS

Reading books he's made by himself or ones made by Mom or Dad is one of the most rewarding activities your child can experience. You'll watch him delight in reading them again and again, to you, himself, or even a stuffed toy. Invite friends and family to listen. Tape record his achievement. He'll treasure original books as special friends.

CHAPTER 8

Reading "Real" Books
"I CAN READ ALL BY MYSELF"

WHAT ARE "REAL" BOOKS?

Just ask your child what "real" books are. She'll probably tell you they're the books you buy from a store, check out from the library, or get as a gift from Grandma. They're the ones she sees you read and the ones you read aloud to her.

By reading aloud to your child, you've already opened the door to this wonderful world of books. Her enjoyment of the tales you've shared contained within the covers of books make her eager to experience them on her own. The personalized reading materials and experiences you've

provided will allow your child to "crack" the stories real books contain.

This chapter will reaffirm that there's no better way to learn to read than to read material of vital interest. And the best source for that material, along with books you and your child make, is children's literature. The children's book industry is exploding with irresistible trade books on every imaginable topic and story, both classic and new. Never has there been a better time to be a beginning reader. How fortunate your child is!

STAGES OF DEVELOPMENT

First let's look at the stages of reading development as they apply to reading real books. Typically children are labeled as "readers" or "non-readers." These labels imply that children either have absolutely no reading ability or they can read. On the contrary, we've seen how learning to read is a gradual process that begins at birth with the child's first attempts to find meaning in her world. Children who cannot yet read the words in a book may still know much about the process. They may know letter sounds. They may be able to identify favorite words and environmental print. They may be familiar with the sound of written language, having heard stories and rhymes read aloud.

To understand how children become readers, we will call those children who are not yet able to read print on their own, *beginning readers*, and then, *developing readers*. We'll call those who can read, *independent readers*. Children at each stage have some degree of understanding of what reading is about. Although all children seem to progress through these stages, they do so at their own rate and in their own style. There are no rules governing how long children should or do remain at each stage. Children will most certainly exhibit characteristics from more than one stage at a time.

THE BEGINNING READER

She senses that the spoken language she hears corresponds to the printed words on a page. During read-aloud time, she may chime in on a familiar refrain or the predictable last word of a sentence. She enjoys a book on her own by using picture clues to retell a story that has already been read aloud to her.

 THE DEVELOPING READER

She associates meaning with print. She understands the concept that spoken language is made up of separate words that can be written down in a unique way. She is able to identify words in her environment as well as words she sees repeated throughout a story. She has a storehouse of special words, important to her, that she can read at first sight. She understands letter sounds and uses the first sound of a printed word along with picture and story clues to identify the word. She can read a refrain during a read-aloud story. She can read predictable words at the end of a passage you have read aloud.

As her abilities develop, she can follow along and read much of the print on the page of a familiar book. She is learning to read more of the text independently.

 THE INDEPENDENT READER

She knows how to read. She puts together a variety of reading strategies to make sense of print. She determines what makes sense in terms of the meaning of the rest of the sentence, language structure, and letter sounds to figure out unknown words. Although it's easier for her to read familiar stories, she has begun to read books that have never been read aloud to her before. She can read books aloud to a younger sibling. She is "book wise" and enjoys discussing favorite stories and characters with you.

SUPPORTING THE READING PROCESS

Print effortlessly melts into meaning for the fluent reader. She comfortably enjoys the unfolding of ideas. Understanding print only comes when language flows. If children are struggling to figure out each word, they can not keep track of the meaning. If reading becomes a frustrating exercise in word-cracking instead of story-cracking, children give up. Therefore, all children, including beginning and developing readers must experience this effortless melting of print into meaning if they are to be successful.

How is this possible for children who don't yet possess the necessary skills to decipher print? You make it happen with your interaction (see *Guided Learning*, page 16). Whether you are the *model* for the beginning reader by reading aloud, the *supporter* for the developing reader by reading along with her, or the *consultant* for the independent reader by carefully selecting a book unique to her interests, you allow each to experience the magic of fluency regardless of her stage of development. Help your child gain fluency with these strategies for each stage of development.

THE READER AT EACH STAGE

Keep reading vital to the pursuit of her interests.

- Tune in to your child's interests and offer her books too good to resist. Remember, the more she wants to read, the better reader she becomes.
- Offer reading material that you've already read aloud for independent reading. Let her read by herself, secure and confident in the book's familiarity.
- Ask her questions and remind her of experiences that help her to relate the story or information to her own life.
- Involve your child in book selection.
- Use the same read-aloud techniques to warm her up before she reads, keep her interested as she reads, and invite reaction to the story after she reads (see *How to Begin* and *Transferring Strategies*, chapter 4).
- Encourage repeated reading of the same material. Practice makes perfect and reading becomes more comfortable and enjoyable.

 THE BEGINNING READER

Help your child solidify the connection between print and meaning.

- Follow along with your finger as you read aloud.
- Give special attention to refrains by reading them aloud together as you follow the words with your finger.
- Allow her to say the refrain by herself. Point to each printed word with your finger as she says it. This helps her match the words she knows with those she sees in print.
- Leave out the predictable words at the ends of sentences and let her say them as you point to them.
- Point out and let her read particularly interesting words (such as *Goldilocks* or *Trip, trap, trip, trap*) that might repeat throughout the story as you read aloud.
- Figure out the story of a wordless book together. Then let her retell it by herself.
- Retell a story you've read aloud, showing her how picture clues help to recall the story.
- Encourage her to retell a favorite story to you as she turns the pages of her book.

THE DEVELOPING READER

Help her reading flow easily so she can comprehend and enjoy what she reads.

- Pick reading material where at least 95 percent of the words are known to your child. This may mean you use one-word or one-sentence books. Or, your child may practice reading just the refrain portion of a pattern book. Reading should not be a test of endurance.
- Read aloud at the same time your child reads aloud, adjusting your pace to hers. Model expressiveness and continuous language flow as you read. As her ability develops, allow her to read easy passages aloud on her own. Join in again if the material becomes difficult. With this technique, you provide an immediate model for correct reading.
- Try "echo reading" where you read a sentence and your child reads it right after you.
- Take turns reading aloud and pointing to the print for each other.

 THE INDEPENDENT READER

Strengthen her reading ability and enrich her enjoyment by helping her discover deeper meaning in what she reads:

- Share personal experiences that relate to the book.
- Encourage her to talk or write about the book. She might like to write or tell her own version of the story or ending of the story. She may enjoy retelling or rewriting the story as if she were the main character.
- Invite your child's participation during read-aloud time. You can take turns reading sentences, paragraphs, or pages. You'll provide an immediate model of flowing, written language read aloud, as she practices her new skill.
- Make reading time theater time. Let your child read the hero's dialogue while you read the narration and dialogue of other characters.

DEALING WITH ERRORS

Correcting reading errors involves striking a delicate balance between teaching the mechanics of the process and retaining interest in the story. The enjoyment of the story is foremost, but sharing strategies for figuring out unknown words helps your child gain reading independence. Use your intuition. Avoid belaboring the point. And try the techniques below:

- Pick reading material where at least 95 percent of the words are known. Familiar books foster error-free reading.
- Only correct errors that affect the meaning of the sentence. If the word is *mother* and your child says "mommy," make no comment. If she says "monster," correct the word.
- Tell your child most words she is unable to figure out within five seconds. This will limit her anxiety and free her to follow the story.
- Suggest your child get a "running start" on the word by beginning the sentence again.
- If not knowing the word won't affect her understanding, suggest she skip it for now and figure it out at a break in the story.
- Ask, "Does that word make sense? What word would?"
- Encourage your child to sound out just the first letter and think about what word would make sense. If more information is needed, help your child sound out the entire word.
- Sometimes help your child figure out unknown words. Demonstrate techniques of sounding the word or first letter out (phonics), and/or using picture or story (meaning) clues, and/or sentence (structure) clues. Reread *The Reading Process* in chapter 1 to clarify how fluent readers figure out unknown words.
- Once the word is figured out, have your child reread the entire sentence to recover its meaning.

TRADE BOOKS FOR EACH READING STAGE

Offering your child the right trade book at the right stage allows her to read successfully on her own. Even the beginning reader can enjoy independent "reading" with a wordless picture book. The following recommended books encourage your child to practice her new skills within the security of written language appropriate for her ability. This is not to suggest that children should only interact with books they can read independently. Make a wide range of books available, while emphasizing those most appropriate for independent reading practice.

Think back to how your baby learned to speak. Not only was she exposed to the simple words she could fully understand, she also heard sophisticated language among adults and children, stories, songs, poems, voices on television, radio, and audio recordings. So, too, your child needs to interact with varied and vast amounts of reading material. She needs to continue to listen to stories read aloud that would be too difficult for her to read. She needs to continue reading easy books to practice her budding fluency. Nonfiction, joke books, magazines, catalogs, guide books — any reading material she enjoys will contribute to her reading competency.

Also, your child benefits from experiencing the same book at different stages of development. As a beginning reader she listens to the story read aloud and retells it by herself. As a developing reader she reads the refrain. And as an independent reader, she reads the entire story on her own. You'll get maximum reading mileage from carefully selected books!

Please note that the following books promote independent reading. See chapter 4 for recommended types of read-alouds.

 THE BEGINNING READER

Wordless picture books are perfect for the beginner. Their rich illustrations contain enough information to allow independent understanding of a story contained in a real book. *One-word* or *one-sentence books* introduce the connection between a picture concept and a printed word. *Alphabet books* promote an awareness of letter sounds. Your child sees how words beginning with the same sound are categorized together. *Predictable books, books of chants, songs, and rhymes*, used as read-togethers, help the beginning reader become instantly familiar with the patterns of printed language. She can then match the words of a known refrain with the print she sees on the page.

 THE DEVELOPING READER

One-word and *one-sentence books* give the developing reader confidence. She can use picture clues along with a basic understanding of letter sounds to figure out what the simple text says. The very structure of *predictable books* and those of *chants, songs, and rhymes* supports the developing reader through the story, allowing her to read independently. Often there is a refrain your child has already memorized that repeats throughout the story. *Controlled-vocabulary readers* build sight vocabulary with their frequent repetition of few words.

 THE INDEPENDENT READER

Now she's ready for *picture story books*. There's nothing more inviting than a beautifully illustrated picture book. With few sentences on a page, picture books look deceptively easy to read. Yet, if carefully selected, their vocabulary is rich and their stories deep. They are welcoming, yet challenging. Start out by offering your child her favorite read-alouds for independent reading. If she's already familiar with the story, she'll amaze you by reading them — hard words and all. Soon she'll be reading new books comfortably at first sight. Then it's on to *short chapter books* and *novels*.

IDENTIFYING PREDICTABLE BOOKS

Predictable books, mentioned above, are particularly important to offer to your child. They support her through the reading process because their words can easily be anticipated. Many are included in chapter 9, the *Treasury*. The characteristics of these special books are listed below so you can identify more of them at the bookstore or library. Predictable books will have one or more of these characteristics:

 RHYTHM AND RHYME

The poetry of the language makes the words predictable. *Dr. Seuss books; nursery rhymes.*

 REPETITION

A word, sentence, refrain, or event repeats throughout the story. *Little Red Hen; The Gingerbread Man.*

 ONE THING LEADS TO ANOTHER

Each event causes the next. *If You Give a Mouse a Cookie; Fortunately.*

 TIME SEQUENCE

Events follow a natural time chronology. *Pumpkin, Pumpkin; The Very Hungry Caterpillar.*

 CHAINING

Events accumulate and are repeated. *The House that Jack Built; The Old Lady Who Swallowed a Fly.*

 FAMILIARITY

The plot or characters' actions occur in a way your child can easily relate to. *Someday; Mr. Gumpy's Outing.*

These characteristics are why predictable books practically read themselves. Children almost instantly experience what reading fluency feels like. Children develop confidence and the mind-set that, "I can read all by myself!"

INDEPENDENT READING — THE ULTIMATE GOAL

Empowering your child with independent reading ability is your ultimate goal. With reading independence comes the ability to learn about anything your child desires, at any time, without depending on others. She has unlimited access to a world of information and entertainment. The power of literacy is evident when we remember how withholding print and literacy have been used historically to repress groups of people. Literacy truly is the path to freedom.

Encouraging your child to read independently goes a long way to instilling the life-long reading habit. It won't work to say to your child, "Now it's time for you to read by yourself." Your child may perceive such a demand as a rejection and firmly resist. Instead, set the stage for

independent reading to just happen. No matter what your child's reading ability, you can encourage her to read on her own.

- Pique independent interest in books by reading aloud.
- Set out the books you've read aloud for your child to explore on her own.
- Offer toddlers and babies board books to explore.
- Provide extra time after you've read aloud a bedtime story for your child to enjoy some favorites on her own.
- Compile a stack of familiar favorites and place them where your child plays.
- Invite your child to read her own books and magazines while other family members relax and read newspapers, magazines, or books.

TAKING STOCK

At this point, your child is simultaneously developing thinking, language, reading, and writing skills. Keep the process child-centered and fun.

 ### DO EVERYTHING AT ONCE

Remember, skills are learned simultaneously. Don't wait until your child speaks perfectly before you offer her books. And don't wait until she can read before you encourage her to write. Instead, no matter what her ability level, offer continual opportunities to listen, speak, read, and write. Your child can learn words phonetically, at the same time she learns special words by sight. She can read the material you've made for her, as well as many kinds of trade books. Invite her full interaction with all aspects of spoken and written language right from the start!

 ### LET YOUR CHILD TAKE THE LEAD

It's more important to follow your child playfully than the instructions precisely. If your child isn't interested in an activity, forget it for now. If she wants to make a birthday card when you're preparing to read her a book, go with her choice. If she enjoys learning special words more than sounding out words, let her do so. She'll best learn what interests her.

 ### HAVE FUN

Repeat appealing activities. Don't feel they must be mastered at once or all variations tried. Let your child become comfortable with the many new skills she's learning. Take time to review, letting her be successful at what she already knows before continuing. There is no optimal number of special words or new songs to learn. Let your child experience as much oral and written language as she enjoys.

WHERE TO GO FROM HERE

Your young child has taken some remarkable steps. She now understands that print is a form of language communication in which she can participate. Her thinking skills have sharpened, and her language has blossomed. She can express her own thoughts in writing. She knows that letters represent sounds she can blend to form meaningful words. And perhaps most exciting to her, she can read books!

Keep up the momentum by offering reading material that's just too good to turn down. Remember, the more she reads, the better reader she'll become, and the more she'll enjoy reading.

The books you've personalized have become springboards for delving into "real" books. The *Treasury*, in chapter 9, serves as a guide to resources that help your child make a smooth transition to independent reading. By continuing to read aloud, you whet her appetite for an incredible world of knowledge, fantasy, and adventure. The only problem you may have is keeping your home stocked with enough books, so visit the library frequently, perhaps purchasing those books that become particular favorites.

Just think, your child is becoming a capable and enthusiastic reader because you've offered opportunities that let her naturally grow up reading!

CHAPTER 9

The Treasury for Literacy Independence

RESOURCES THAT HELP BEGINNERS BECOME CAPABLE AND ENTHUSIASTIC USERS OF PRINT

SELECTION

The Treasury for Literacy Independence is a guide to books and other materials that will help children move confidently from beginning to independent reading and writing ability. The suggested books, magazines, manipulative materials, writing resources, audio recordings, and computer software allow children to explore and celebrate the many forms of written and spoken language. Parent/teacher resources are also included to allow you to make the most of the ever-changing world of technology and media for your child. The opportunities these materials offer can help children become capable and enthusiastic users of print.

The books included in *The Treasury* were selected with the following criteria in mind. They are:

 IRRESISTIBLE

The books reaffirm reading's importance to the pursuit of children's interests. They stimulate their minds and imaginations. They present the familiar as well as offer new perspectives. They deal with the imaginary and real; the past and present; neighborhoods like theirs and ones from around the world. There are folk tales and new tales. There are characters who solve problems in positive ways. Nonfiction is included to satisfy children's curiosity to learn all they can about their world. The books are appealing with rich and attractive illustrations.

 LANGUAGE-RICH

Even books offered for the beginner have outstanding literary value. The rich language and captivating plots are those of master storytellers. There are opportunities to learn new vocabulary words as well as practice the known. Books offer exposure to quality language that not only enriches children's reading ability, but also serves as a model for their writing.

 EASY-TO-READ

Each book has several of the following elements that support the beginning reader through the text: large text, rhyming words, refrains, repeating words, predictable plots, and/or pictures that give good clues as to what's happening. As children become more fluent, they'll require fewer of these elements to carry them through the story.

NEVER TOO MANY OPPORTUNITIES

This listing is by no means complete. Look for more books by your child's favorite authors. Excellent books often go out of print, so some of these listings may only be available in your library. Use the above criteria as a guide for making your own book selections. Keep in mind that the number one criterion is your child's enthusiasm for the book.

With your child's insatiable appetite for stories, information, and learning activities, you can never offer too many opportunities to interact with print!

BOARD BOOKS

Indestructible books are a must for babies who like to chew whatever they get their hands on. Supplement these books with plenty of destructible catalogs and magazines to encourage the wonderful experience of turning a real page.

ALL FALL DOWN • CLAP HANDS • SAY GOODNIGHT • TICKLE, TICKLE
by Helen Oxenbury
Macmillan
Romp across the pages with these very playful baby friends.

I AM A LITTLE:
CAT • DOG • ELEPHANT • LION • PIG
by Francois Crozat
Barron's
Realistic, detailed drawings show the fascinating daily exploits of young animals. Many titles available in tiny formats for on-the-go enjoyment.

LODESTAR NURSERY RHYMES:
BAA, BAA, BLACK SHEEP • HEY DIDDLE DIDDLE • HICKORY DICKORY DOCK • THIS LITTLE PIGGY
Dutton
Perfect for sharing or enjoying alone. Clear text and illustrations let even the youngest children follow along with their favorite songs.

LOOK AT ME BOOKS:
LOOK AT ME • BATHTIME • MEALTIME • PLAYTIME
photos by Stephen Shott
Dutton
Bright, descriptive photographs of babies just being themselves.

PANDA, PANDA • RED, BLUE, YELLOW SHOE • WHAT IS IT?
by Tana Hoban
Greenwillow
Vivid photography introduces simple concepts and words.

PAT THE BUNNY
by Dorothy Kunhardt
PAT THE CAT
by Edith Kunhardt
Golden
Filled with sensorial delights from feeling Daddy's beard to petting Pat. (Less durable than other listings.)

POKE AND LOOK BOOKS:
I AM AN OWL • LAND OF COLOR • ONE GREEN FROG • WHEELS GO ROUND
Grosset and Dunlap
Cutout concentric shapes add an intriguing tactile experience to these books.

SPOT LOOKS AT SHAPES • SPOT ON THE FARM • SPOT'S FIRST WORDS
by Eric Hill
Putnam
Bright, bold, basic. A lovable puppy befriends your baby.

WHAT ELSE COULD IT BE? • WHAT'S HIDING • WHAT'S MISSING • WHAT WILL IT BE?
by Mario Gamboli
Boyd Mills
Cutout pages build on children's curiosity and encourage plenty of exploration.

WORDLESS BOOKS

Children gather meaning from the pictures, then supply the language for the story. These books offer the chance to independently experience the great companionship of a book.

A BEAR AND THE FLY
by Paula Winter
Crown
How much trouble can a tiny fly cause? Invite one to a bear family's dinner and see.

A BOY, A DOG, AND A FROG • FROG GOES TO DINNER • FROG ON HIS OWN • FROG, WHERE ARE YOU?
by Mercer Mayer
Dial
Warm, humorous tales about a boy and his unpredictable pet.

CARL GOES SHOPPING • GOOD DOG CARL
by Alexandra Day
Green Tiger
An infant and her canine baby-sitter share fun times while Mom's away. Beautifully depicted. More stories available in the series.

DEEP IN THE FOREST
by Brinton Turkle
Dutton
The story of Goldilocks from a different point of view: Baby Bear visits her house. Detailed pictures let your child tell this charming version.

DREAMS • NOAH'S ARK • PETER SPIER'S RAIN
by Peter Spier
Doubleday
Dream along with two imaginative cloud gazers on a lazy warm afternoon. Or help Noah prepare for the Great Flood. Then, enjoy a day of discovery in the rain. Experience it all through the paint, pen, and ink of a gifted children's illustrator.

THE HUNTER AND THE ANIMALS
Holiday
PANCAKES FOR BREAKFAST
Harcourt; Scholastic
by Tomie DePaola
The first book tells how a lost hunter is helped by the very animals he had intended to shoot. Realizing friendship, he breaks his gun. In the second, an old lady's plans for making pancakes are foiled by her hungry pets. But she still finds a way to eat pancakes!

MOONLIGHT • SUNSHINE
by Jan Ormerod
Lothrop; Puffin
A young girl's routines of going to sleep and getting up in the morning become adventures every child can relate to.

PADDY'S EVENING OUT • THE MIDNIGHT ADVENTURES OF KELLY, DOT, AND ESMERALDA
by John S. Goodall
McElderry
Half pages uniquely create a sense of action in these old-time British adventures.

THE SNOWMAN
by Raymond Briggs
Random
Lovely images illustrate the magical relationship between a boy and his come-to-life snowman.

UP AND UP
by Shirley Hughes
Lothrop
Everyone dreams of flying. Follow this child from her first taste of a magic egg to an amazing flight that startles everyone in town.

WE HIDE, YOU SEEK
by Jose Aruego and Ariane Dewey
Morrow
Visit East Africa while searching with rhino for camouflaged animals.

WHERE'S MY MONKEY?
by Dieter Schubert
Dial
A pleasant outing turns into disaster when a boy's favorite stuffed toy disappears. How he gets his monkey back is an amazing story.

ONE-WORD OR ONE-SENTENCE BOOKS

An introduction to the world of print. Children learn how words enhance the meaning of the pictures. Pictures provide the clues for discovering what the words say.

AIRPORT
Harper
DINOSAURS, DINOSAURS
Scholastic
by Byron Barton
Bold pictures and print capture the excitement of these favorite topics.

**ALL CLEAN! • ALL GONE! • COCK-A-DOODLE-DOO!
• RUN! RUN!**
Harper
THE BATH BOOK • THE BED BOOK
Scholastic
by Harriet Ziefert
Bold illustrations and fun vocabulary make this first group of books a delight to read. Daily routines become fun times in the second group of books.

THE BABY'S CATALOGUE
by Janet and Allan Ahberg
Atlantic
The orderly catalogue format satisfies a young child's fascination with the world of babies.

BABY'S WORLD • EL MUNDO DEL BEBE
Dorling Kindersley
Brilliant photos catalog baby's world. The book is available in English or Spanish.

CAROUSEL • HARBOR • LIGHT
Greenwillow
FREIGHT TRAIN • PARADE • SCHOOL BUS • TRUCK
Scholastic
by Donald Crews
Simple, striking illustrations and brief captions bring these entities alive.

CAT ON THE MAT • THE ISLAND • THE NEST
by Brian Wildsmith
Oxford
Beautifully illustrated pages with or without a few simple words.

DON'T FORGET THE BACON! • ONE HUNTER
Greenwillow
ROSIE'S WALK
Macmillan; Scholastic
by Pat Hutchins
In the first book, a chanted shopping list evolves into an exotic collection of things to buy. The second is an animal counting story: See if you're more observant than the hunter. In the third, Rosie the hen easily outfoxes the fox. Suspense is created with few words.

**FARMYARD SOUNDS • I'M NOT SLEEPY!
• JUNGLE SOUNDS • WHERE'S MOMMY?**
by Colin and Jacqui Hawkins
Crown
Your child will enjoy making animal sounds in the first two books. Then he'll giggle as he reads the next two "comic books" designed for beginning readers.

FEATHERS FOR LUNCH
by Lois Ehlert
Harcourt
Follow a cat in her unsuccessful quest for a fresh, wild meal. Meet and learn about the lunch (12 colorful birds) that got away.

**GROWTH • MOTION • SHAPES • SOUNDS
• TOOLS • TOUCH**
by Eric Carle
Crowell
Split cardboard pages let your child match the top half of the page with the corresponding word or picture on the bottom half. Single words or wordless.

GUINEA PIGS FAR AND NEAR
by Kate Duke
Dutton
Guinea pigs help your child learn concepts. Each concept is brightly illustrated and defined with a single word.

HAVE YOU SEEN MY DUCKLING?
by Nancy Tafuri
Greenwillow; Scholastic
This award-winning book tells of a mother's love and a child's independence. Count the ducklings on each page. Then, find the missing one. Also, available in Spanish.

**HOW DO I PUT IT ON? • I CAN BUILD A HOUSE
• I CAN RIDE IT!**
by Shigo Watanabe
Philomel
This large-print book features a lovable bear who helps your child read and learn simple concepts.

**I CAN DRESS MYSELF • I CAN READ
• I CAN READ MORE**
by Dick Bruna
Price Stern Sloan
Picture clues and large print assure reading success. Boldly colored illustrations are uniquely Bruna's.

IN THE TALL, TALL GRASS
by Denise Fleming
Scholastic
A fuzzy little caterpillar takes you on an amazing journey through the tall, tall grass.

I READ SIGNS
by Tana Hoban
Greenwillow
Outstanding photography brings functional words off the streets and into your home. Hoban has authored and illustrated many concept books with her unique photographs.

JAFTA
by Hugh Lewin
Carolrhoda
*Set in Africa, this book of similes makes a nice companion to **Quick as a Cricket**.*

A MOUSE IN THE HOUSE: A REAL-LIFE GAME OF HIDE AND SEEK
by Henrietta
Dorling Kindersley
Find Henrietta Mouse as she scurries through food, clothing, hardware . . . everywhere!

MY FIRST LOOK AT BOOKS: COLORS • HOME • NATURE • NUMBERS • OPPOSITES • SEASONS • SHAPES • SIZES • TOUCH
Random House
Beautiful photographic books that label and organize everyday objects into exciting categories.

MY FIRST WORD BOOK
Dorling Kindersley
One thousand very important objects in a child's life, all exquisitely photographed and thematically categorized.

PEEK-A-BOOKS: ANIMALS • FAIRY TALES • OPPOSITES • WHAT'S THAT?
by Eric Hill
Price Stern Sloan
A child's trivia series with each page posing a question. Look under the pop-up flap for the answer.

RAIN
by Robert Kalan
Greenwillow
A storm builds through easy-to-remember text and bold illustrations.

SKATES!
by Ezra Jack Keats
Watts
Single words punctuate the frustrations and rewards of skating.

SPOT GOES TO THE BEACH • SPOT'S FIRST WALK • WHERE'S SPOT?
by Eric Hill
Putnam
A lovable puppy and large print make these enormously popular books ideal for very beginning readers. Every page has a flap hiding someone or something and a fun-to-read dialogue balloon. Many Spot titles are available in Spanish and in a tiny take-along size.

WHERE'S DADDY'S CAR? • WHERE'S MOMMY'S TRUCK?
by Harriet Ziefert
Harper
Even the youngest reader can participate by reading and lifting flaps to find these errant vehicles.

WORMS WIGGLE
by David Pelham and Michael Foreman
Simon and Schuster
An action-packed pop-up book even a beginner can enjoy.

CHANTS, SONGS, AND RHYMES

Chants, songs, and rhymes let children read with ease because the material is familiar. Oral language and reading flow with simultaneous singing or chanting and reading.

ALLIGATOR PIE
by Dennis Lee
Macmillan (Canada)
A unique collection of modern nursery rhymes. The fun rhythms and rhymes invite children to create their own versions.

ALL THE PRETTY HORSES
by Susan Jeffers
Scholastic
Dream-like paintings illustrate this favorite lullaby.

ANNA BANANA: 101 JUMP-ROPE RHYMES
Beech Tree Books; Scholastic
THE EENTSY WEENTSY SPIDER: FINGER PLAYS AND ACTION RHYMES • MISS MARY MACK AND OTHER CHILDREN'S STREET RHYMES
Mulberry
by Joanna Cole and Stephanie Calmenson
Complete instructions and words for all your favorites. You'll never be rhymeless again!

ARROZ CON LECHE
by Lulu Delacre
Scholastic
A wonderful collection of Hispanic nursery rhymes.

BROADWAY BANJO BILL • SHOESHINE SHIRLEY
by Leah Komaiko
Doubleday
Those who love rap will delight in these toe-tapping rhymes. Bold and comical illustrations.

BROWN BEAR, BROWN BEAR, WHAT DO YOU SEE? POLAR BEAR, POLAR BEAR, WHAT DO YOU HEAR?
by Bill Martin, Jr.
Holt
CHICKA CHICKA BOOM BOOM
by Bill Martin and John Archambault
Simon and Schuster
The first two books practically read themselves with their powerful rhythm and predictable language. Your child can easily add verses to make these never-ending stories. The last is the jazziest alphabet book around.

DANCE AWAY • LIZARD'S SONG
by George Shannon
Greenwillow
The rhythmic songs that repeat throughout these tales delight young children and invite their participation.

EACH PEACH PEAR PLUM
by Janet and Allan Ahberg
Scholastic
A clever version of "I spy" with nursery rhyme characters hidden on each page.

FATHER GANDER'S NURSERY RHYMES
by Douglas Larche
Advocacy
The spirit of equality is captured in this charming remake of Mother Goose. All children feel proud as Little Boy Blue blows his horn and Little Girl Green sounds the alarm. Poems model the concept of creating original versions from classics.

FISH EYES: A BOOK YOU CAN COUNT ON
by Lois Ehlert
Harcourt
A brilliant underwater counting book.

FOX WENT OUT ON A CHILLY NIGHT
illustrated by Peter Spier
Doubleday
The thrilling nighttime exploits of roguish Mr. Fox. Fox families need to eat, too! ". . . and the little ones chewed on the bones-o, bones-o, bones-o." Other nursery rhymes illustrated by Spier are published by Dell.

I KNOW AN OLD LADY WHO SWALLOWED A FLY •
OLD MOTHER HUBBARD
illustrated by Colin and Jacqui Hawkins
Putnam
What fun to lift up the old lady's skirt to see what goes down the hatch. Or, open the door to see what Mother Hubbard's crazy dog is up to. Zany retellings of classic rhymes.

I WENT WALKING
by Sue Williams
Harcourt
Simple rhythmic text makes the book a snap to read.

IS YOUR MAMA A LLAMA?
by Deborah Guarino
Scholastic
Rhythmic words assure your child can joyfully answer each riddle as he learns about animal families. Joyfully illustrated by Steven Kellogg. Also available in Spanish.

IT'S ABOUT TIME, JESSE BEAR AND OTHER RHYMES • JESSE BEAR, WHAT WILL YOU WEAR?
by Nancy Carlstrom
Macmillan
Charming rhymes about a charming bear.

JAMBERRY
by Bruce Degen
Harper, Scholastic
What could be more fun than a rhyming romp through piles and fields of every imaginable type of berry?

THE KEYS TO MY KINGDOM: A POEM IN THREE LANGUAGES
by Lydia Dabcovich
Lothrop
What are the keys to your child's kingdom? For this child, they are paint and brushes. Classic poem, imaginatively illustrated.

KIDS
by Catherine and Laurence Anhold
Candlewick Press
All you ever wanted to know about kids told through rollicking rhyme and joyous illustrations.

A LIGHT IN THE ATTIC • WHERE THE SIDEWALK ENDS
by Shel Silverstein
Harper
The zaniest rhymes you'll ever find. Enjoyable for all ages through adulthood.

MARY HAD A LITTLE LAMB
by Sarah Josepha Hale
illustrated by Tomie DePaola
Holiday
photographed by Bruce Macmillan
Scholastic
Compare and contrast these two interpretations of a classic nursery favorite.

MOONBEAM ON A CAT'S EAR • RAINY DAY MAGIC
by Marie-Louise Gay
Stoddart (Canada)
Come along with Rosie and Toby as they pull the moon right out of the sky. Then, venture to "a place where banana trees sway and on to a slippery slide on a snake's scaly gown." All told in rhyme. Imaginatively illustrated.

MOTHER GOOSE
illustrated by Aurelius Battaglia
Random
A budget-priced edition with clear text and bright pictures.

MOTHER GOOSE: A COLLECTION OF CLASSIC NURSERY RHYMES
illustrated by Michael Hague
Holt
Exquisite full-color paintings and large, readable text.

THE NEW BABY CALF
by Edith Newlin Chase
Scholastic
This gentle poem comes to life through unique plasticine images by Canadian artist Barbara Reid. Plenty of repeated phrases make this book fun and easy to read.

THE NEW KID ON THE BLOCK • SOMETHING BIG HAS BEEN HERE
by Jack Prelutsky
Greenwillow; Scholastic
Whimsical poems to delight your child. Expect the unexpected!

NOISY NORA
by Rosemary Wells
Dial; Scholastic
Nora finds a way to make her busy family pay attention.

NOISY POEMS
collected by Jill Bennett
Oxford
The perfect poetry collection for connoisseurs of "clickety-clack, zoomba-zoom, or slosh a goulash."

NORTHERN LIGHT
by Nancy Carlstrom
Philomel
*A version of **Goodnight, Moon** from the far north. Breathtaking illustrations.*

OVER IN THE MEADOW
by Olive Wadsworth
Scholastic
This classic Southern Appalachian counting rhyme comes to life through Ezra Jack Keats' charming illustrations.

THE OWL AND THE PUSSYCAT
by Edward Lear
Scholastic
Jan Brett's rich illustrations give this amusing poem a special interpretation.

RAFFI SONGS TO READ: BABY BELUGA • DOWN BY THE BAY • THE WHEELS ON THE BUS
Crown
This popular children's entertainer creates a bridge between singing and reading with easy-to-follow books of favorite songs.

SHEEP IN A JEEP • SHEEP IN A SHOP • SHEEP ON A SHIP • SHEEP OUT TO EAT
by Nancy Shaw
Houghton Mifflin
Join in the antics of unruly sheep. Rich vocabulary in rhyme makes these books simple to read.

SHOES
by Elizabeth Winthrop
Harper
Warmly illustrated rhyme about the marvels of a kid's most prized possession.

TEDDY BEARS' PICNIC
by Jimmy Kennedy
Green Tiger
Detailed tempera paintings offer a special interpretation of this delightful song. Includes a record with two classic versions. Great fun!

TEN, NINE, EIGHT
by Molly Bang
Greenwillow
A bedtime ritual becomes a counting rhyme.

WE'RE GOING ON A BEAR HUNT
retold by Michael Rosen
McElderry; Macmillan
Chant along with this classic story as you travel through oozy mud, a swirling snowstorm, and more, to meet . . . a bear!

WHERE'S MY TEDDY?
by Jez Alborough
Candlewick
A case of mistaken Teddy bear identity will keep your child at the edge of his seat!

VOCABULARY-CONTROLLED BEGINNING READING SERIES

A limited vocabulary repeats throughout these books so children can read stories with familiar words. Stories are often told in rhyme to help predict the words. Large print also aids readability. The individual titles within each series are too numerous to mention, and the list grows yearly. Your child will probably outgrow these books long before he's read them all.

ALL ABOARD READING
Grosset Dunlap

BANK STREET READY-TO-READ
The Rebus Bears
by Seymour Reit
Bank Street
*This particularly unique book in the series uses rebus clues to guide young readers through **Goldilocks and the Three Bears**.*

BEGINNER BOOKS
ARE YOU MY MOTHER? • GO, DOG, GO
by P. D. Eastman
GREEN EGGS AND HAM •HOP ON POP
by Dr. Seuss

IN A PEOPLE'S HOUSE
by Theo. LeSieg
Random
These favorites that may have helped you learn to read can teach your child rhyme, sight words, and phonics.

BEGINNING-TO-READ BOOKS • JUST-BEGINNING-TO-READ BOOKS
Modern Curriculum

BREAK OF DAY • NATE THE GREAT
by Marjorie Sharmat
Coward

BRIGHT AND EARLY BOOKS • BEGINNER BOOKS
Random

DIAL EASY-TO-READ BOOKS
Dial

DISNEY'S WONDERFUL WORLD OF READING
Random

EARLY I CAN READ BOOKS • I CAN READ BOOKS FROG AND TOAD TOGETHER • MOUSE TALES
by Arnold Lobel
DANNY AND THE DINOSAUR • JULIUS • SAMMY THE SEAL
by Syd Hoff
LITTLE BEAR
by Else Minarik
Harper
HELLO READER
Scholastic

HELLO READING
Puffin

HENRY AND MUDGE BOOKS
by Cynthia Rylant
Aladdin

I CAN READ BOOKS AND CASSETTES
Caedmon Audio
*Book and cassette packages for some of the titles in the **Early I Can Read** and **I Can Read** series listed above.*

A JUST ONE MORE BOOK • MY FIRST READER
Children's Press

LADYBIRD BOOKS
***Ladybirds** have long encouraged British and Montessori school children to read. Every imaginable topic is covered and classic tale told — for every age and ability level. Their small size is perfect for little hands. **Ladybirds** are organized into many series.*

*   **Read It Yourself** presents classic stories at varying ability levels. While **Sly Fox and Red Hen** has one or two sentences per page, **Heidi** features full pages of text. Although the overall vocabulary and sentence structure is controlled, additional descriptive words necessary for communicating the story are readily used.*

*   The detailed illustrations of **Talkabouts** provide a perfect springboard for discussing such topics as bedtime, shopping, and starting school. **First Facts** are information books for young inquiring minds.*

*   **Five Fairy Tales, First Books, First Words, Ready To Read,** and **Early Readers** are all appropriate for beginners.*

*   Ladybird Books can sometimes be found in educational supply stores. Contact the publisher for a catalog and the name of your local distributor of these special British books: Ladybird Books, P.O. Box 1690, Auburn, ME 04210, 800-523-9247.*

PICTUREBACK READERS
Random

READ-ALONE BOOKS
Greenwillow

READ-A-PICTURE BOOKS
Watermill
Rebus books that make learning fun.

READY-TO-READ BOOKS
Macmillan

RED NOSE READERS
Random
These books deserve special recognition for their clever combination of readable pictures and words.

ROOKIE READERS
Children's Press

STEP INTO READING BOOKS
Random

STICKERBOOK READERS
Harper

TEN-WORD READERS
by Patty Wolcott
Random
Complete stories, each told using only ten words.

PICTURE BOOKS

Including Predictable Stories
Captivating illustrations and colorful language typify these books. The engaging stories are told without the limitation of vocabulary control because they are primarily written to be read aloud. However, if your child has heard you read these tales again and again, he'll soon surprise you by reading them by himself, "hard words" and all. The predictable language of many of the following books encourages successful independent reading of refrains, or the entire book.

ABUELA
by Arthur Durros
Dutton
Told in English mixed with Spanish phrases. Imagine flying over Manhattan with your grandma. This book is filled with bright, collage illustrations.

ANIMALS SHOULD DEFINITELY NOT WEAR CLOTHING
by Judi Barrett
Atheneum; Scholastic
The consequences for animals who do wear clothing, told in large, clear text with humorous drawings.

THE BARE NAKED BOOK • BIG OR LITTLE?
• RED IS BEST • THOSE GREEN THINGS
by Kathy Stinson
Annick (Canada)
The first book is a joyful discovery of body parts. The second points out how a child is both big and little. The third uses repeated phrases to explore why red is decidedly the best color. Common green things become slithery snakes or lumpy, bumpy monsters through a child's imagination in the fourth book. All are very predictable.

CAPS FOR SALE
by Esphyr Slobodkina
Harper
The classic tale of a peddler and some mischievous monkeys. Plenty of repetition lets your child participate in reading the story.

THE CARROT SEED • A HOLE IS TO DIG
by Ruth Krauss
Harper; Scholastic
The first book encourages a child to pursue a dream, no matter how discouraging people may be. Also available in Spanish. The second is a book of wonderful definitions, the sort a child might create.

THE CHICK AND THE DUCKLING
by Mirra Ginsburg
Macmillan
A newborn chick wants to do everything his duckling friend does. Even the youngest reader can join in with, "Me, too."

CLIFFORD THE BIG RED DOG
by Norman Bidwell
Scholastic
The ever popular big red dog is all any child could ever dream of in a pet. With tens of books in the series to choose from, Clifford fans won't ever be left without a good dog tale.

COME AWAY FROM THE WATER, SHIRLEY
Harper
MR. GRUMPY'S MOTOR CAR • MR. GRUMPY'S OUTING
Penguin
by John Burningham
In the first book, Shirley's vivid imagination gives her quite a different experience at the beach than what her parents have in mind. Then in the next two, join in the fun of outings with animals that have minds of their own.

"COULD BE WORSE!"
by James Stevenson
Penguin
Grandpa's spine-tingling adventure is a surprising change from his usual "could be worse" attitude.

THE DAY JIMMY'S BOA ATE THE WASH
Dial; Scholastic
JIMMY'S BOA BOUNCES BACK
Dial
by Trinka Hakes Noble
Steven Kellogg's detailed pictures bring alive hilarious havoc all caused by an unwitting boa. The stories unfold through a dialogue between two characters, making these books perfect for shared reading.

DINNER TIME • GOSSIP • LITTLE MONSTERS • SMALL TALK
by Jan Pienkowski
Price Stern Sloan
Colorful and fun pop-up books feature imaginative creatures and large text. Repeating phrases provide a perfect start on independent reading: "I must just tell my friend" or "I'm going to eat you up for my dinner. And he did." Also available in tiny take-along versions.

DO LIKE KYLA • TELL ME A STORY, MAMA
by Angela Johnson
Orchard
Treasured moments of childhood in a Black-American family.

THE DON'T BE SCARED BOOK
by Ilse-Margaret Vogel
Atheneum
Scares and their cures in rhyme with a reassuring refrain for your child to read, "Don't be scared!"

DUNBI THE OWL • ECHIDNA AND THE SHADE TREE • HOW THE BIRDS GOT THEIR COLORS • WHEN THE SNAKE BITES THE SUN
adapted by Pamela Lofts
Mad Hatter
Ancient legends as told by Australian aboriginal tribes to their children. Boldly colored illustrations are adapted from children's paintings of these stories.

EAT!
by Diane Paterson
Dial
Martha wouldn't eat, to the exasperation of her parents. Her nighttime exploits with her pet frog reveal why. Dialogue balloons allow parent and child to each be a character.

FARMER DUCK
by Martin Waddell
Candlewick
The lazy farmer and the hard-working animals get their just rewards. Plenty of animal sounds for participation.

FORTUNATELY
by Remy Charlip
Macmillan
Imagine the good luck of a haystack on the ground beneath you when you're falling from the sky. But what bad luck: a pitchfork in that haystack pointed in your direction. Go from the heights of great fortune to the depths of misfortune just by turning a page.

GEORGE SHRINKS
by William Joyce
Harper; Scholastic
Imagine waking up to find out you are no bigger than a fork. Find out how tiny George copes for a day.

THE GIVING TREE • THE MISSING PIECE
Harper
WHO WANTS A CHEAP RHINOCEROS?
Macmillan
by Shel Silverstein
Silverstein's witty words and illustrations can be enjoyed by beginners.

GOODNIGHT MOON • THE IMPORTANT BOOK • THE RUNAWAY BUNNY
by Margaret Wise Brown
Harper
The first book is the classic tale of a child's bedtime ritual. The second helps us discover "the important things" about what we take for granted. The third tells of a mother bunny's boundless love for her little bunny who insists on running away. It makes for a perfect read-together dialogue.

GRANDFATHER TWILIGHT
Philomel; Scholastic
WHEN THE SUN ROSE
Philomel
by Barbara Berger
Exquisite pictures illuminate the gentleness of twilight and the warmth of friendship.

HAPPY BIRTHDAY, MOON
by Frank Asch
Prentice; Scholastic
A lovable bear and his echo make perfect first reading phrases for you to model and your child to repeat. Asch has written several books about this loveable bear.

HARRY THE DIRTY DOG
by Gene Zion
Harper
Children can identify with this white dog with black spots who hates to take a bath.

IF YOU GIVE A MOOSE A MUFFIN • IF YOU GIVE A MOUSE A COOKIE
by Laura Numeroff
Harper
The consequences for those who do! Perfect springboards for creating your own "if you" stories.

I'M COMING TO GET YOU
by Tony Ross
Dial
This hairy, hungry monster from outer space will keep you on the edge of your seats. Your child can read the only words this monster says, "I'm coming to get you," or read the entire book.

IMOGENE'S ANTLERS
by David Small
Crown; Scholastic
My, how life changes when you wake up with antlers growing on your head.

THE JACKET I WEAR IN THE SNOW
by Shirley Neitzel
Scholastic
A cumulative poem with a rebus verse makes for fun and easy reading.

THE JOKE BOOK • THE RIDDLE BOOK
by Roy McKie
Random
Develop a sense of humor along with reading skill through jokes and riddles that play with language. Take turns asking questions or giving answers.

THE JOLLY POSTMAN OR OTHER PEOPLE'S LETTERS
by Janet and Allan Ahberg
Heinemann
Read a sorry note from Goldilocks or a sale flyer for a wicked witch. A joyful look at print as purposeful communication.

JUMP, FROG, JUMP!
by Robert Kalan
Scholastic
A clever frog and a clever boy give young readers plenty of repeating phrases to read and opportunities to predict what will happen next.

JUST FOR YOU • JUST FOR GRANDMA AND ME • JUST ME AND MY PUPPY
by Mercer Mayer
Western
The trials and tribulations of lovable Little Critter are told with only one sentence per page. Humorous drawings.

THE LITTLE MOUSE, THE RED RIPE STRAWBERRY, AND THE BIG HUNGRY BEAR • QUICK AS A CRICKET
Child's Play
THE NAPPING HOUSE
Harcourt
by Audrey and Don Wood
The first tells of the tremendous responsibility that comes with strawberry ownership. Next is a poem of similes. In the last, a cozy bed is the stage for a peaceful sleep until a wakeful flea sets everyone in motion. All told with incredible illustrations.

A LION IN THE NIGHT
Puffin
WHO SANK THE BOAT?
Coward
by Pamela Allen
First, join the chase about the kingdom for the royal baby and wild lion. Rhythmic, colorful language galore! Next, encourage your child to join in the fun of predicting who sank the boat.

THE LITTLE RED HEN
by Paul Galdone
Houghton Mifflin
Repeating story patterns assure successful reading. Paul Galdone is a great source for other classic tales including: The Three Little Pigs, The Three Billy Goats Gruff, and The Three Bears.

LOVE YOU FOREVER • MORTIMER
by Robert Munsch
Firefly Books (Canada)
Follow a boy's growth from baby to man and learn of the enduring love of parents for children. Then, let your child enjoy repeating sounds along with Mortimer as he infuriates everyone! Refrains repeat throughout both stories.

MADELINE • MADELINE'S RESCUE
by Ludwig Bemelmans
Penguin; Scholastic
Brazen Madeline and a sing-song verse inspire children to read these classics on their own.

THE MAGIC FISH
by Freya Littledale
THE THREE BILLY GOATS GRUFF
illustrated by Allen Appleby
STONE SOUP
by Ann McGovern
Scholastic
Classic folk tales, complete with repeating verses. Attractive, budget-priced cassettes available.

MAMA DON'T ALLOW
by Thatcher Hurd
Harper
This wild tale of an alligator band is fun to read with its many dialogue bubbles.

MAMA, DO YOU LOVE ME?
by Barbara Joose
Scholastic
Set in the Arctic, this read-together tale tells of a child's independence and a mother's unconditional love.

MORE MORE MORE, SAID THE BABY
by Vera B. Williams
Scholastic
A multicultural, multigenerational look at the playful love between babies and their favorite grown-ups.

ONE MONDAY MORNING
by Uri Shulevitz
Scribner
What happens when royal company comes to visit and you're not home. Plenty of repetition for fun and easy reading.

ON MOTHER'S LAP
by Ann Scott
Clarion
There's always room for one more on mother's lap, even when baby sister cries. A reassuring tale set in the home of a Native North American family.

OUR HOME IS IN THE SEA
by Riki Levinson
Puffin
This notable book in the field of Social Studies tells of a young boy's day in the streets and harbor of Hong Kong.

OUTSIDE OVER THERE • WHERE THE WILD THINGS ARE
by Maurice Sendak
Harper
The first book is a beautifully illustrated, mystical tale of a girl's responsibility for her younger sister. A boy fantasizes he is king of the wild things in the second book.

THE PAPER CRANE
by Molly Bang
Mulberry
Set in Japan, this award-winning tale tells of kindness repaid.

PEEPO!
by Janet and Allan Ahlberg
Puffin
A classic that shows us the world through a baby's eyes.

PUMPKIN, PUMPKIN
by Titherington
Scholastic
The simple yet wondrous tale of how a seed eventually becomes a jack-o-lantern.

"QUACK!" SAID THE BILLY-GOAT
by Charles Causley
Harper
Children delight in this farm's mixed-up animals.

READY. . . SET. . . READ
Compiled by Joanne Cole and Stephanie Calmenson
Doubleday
A taste of Lobel, Seuss, Sendak, and more. Enjoy the best of children's literature, stories, poetry, rebuses, and non-fiction, all within one volume.

READ-A-REBUS
by William Hooks et al.
Random
This delightful collection of stories and rhymes invites your child to read pictures, words, and chant refrains.

SAY SOMETHING
by Mary Stolz
Harper
*"Say something about a mountain . . . the moon . . ."
Enjoy these precious moments between a father and son, then try playing your own "say something" game.*

THE SECRET BIRTHDAY MESSAGE
Crowell
THE VERY BUSY SPIDER •
THE VERY HUNGRY CATERPILLAR
by Eric Carle
Philomel; Scholastic
In the first book, a clever message lets readers follow simple shapes and words through cut pages of the book to find a special birthday surprise. In the next book, feel the pages and chant a refrain to learn how a spider spins her web. Then, learn how a caterpillar transforms into a butterfly, the days of the week, and how to count to five.

THE SNOWY DAY
by Ezra Jack Keats
Scholastic; Viking
Uniquely illustrated. The warmth of childhood expressed from a child's point of view.

SUMMER IS . . .
Abelard - Schuman
SOMEDAY
Harper
by Charlotte Zolotow
Discover the special things about each season. Perfect springboard for writing about what your child likes best about summer, winter, spring, and fall. Then enjoy a child's wish book: "Someday when I have nothing to read, the doorbell will ring and a big box of books will come for me." Now add your own someday wishes.

THE STORY OF FERDINAND
by Munro Leaf
Viking; Penguin
This classic tale of nonviolence has withstood the test of time. Everyone loves Ferdinand, the bull who'd rather smell flowers than fight.

TEENY TINY
by Jill Bennett
Putnam
THE TEENY-TINY WOMAN
by Paul Galdone
Houghton Mifflin
Classic ghost tale with a haunting refrain, "Give me back my bone!"

THE THREE LITTLE PIGS AND OTHER FAVORITE NURSERY STORIES
illustrated by Charlotte Voake
Candlewick Press
Ten classics all in one handy volume. Large text, charming illustrations, and the original British versions make this a basic resource no home with young children should be without.

THERE'S A NIGHTMARE IN MY CLOSET
by Mercer Mayer
Dial
What to do if your nightmare is afraid, too!

WHAT DO YOU DO, DEAR? • WHAT DO YOU SAY, DEAR?
by Sesyle Joslin
Harper
WHAT DO YOU DO WITH A KANGAROO?
by Mercer Mayer
Scholastic
Guides for handling various silly and exasperating situations. Perfect read-together books. You read the problem situations, then let your child read the solutions.

WHEN SMALL IS TALL AND OTHER READ TOGETHER TALES
by Seymour V. Reit et al.
Random
Fables teach that little people are important. Plenty of read-together possibilities with dialogue balloons and repeated refrains.

WHERE DOES THE SUN GO AT NIGHT?
by Mirra Ginsburg
Morrow
Based on an Armenian folk song that helps answer this classic child's question.

WHOSE MOUSE ARE YOU?
by Robert Kraus
Scholastic
Question/answer format makes this a perfect read-together tale.

WOLF'S CHICKEN STEW
by Keiko Kasza
Putnam
Cute chicks foil a wolf's plans to fatten their mom up for chicken dinner.

WORKING COTTON
by Sherley Anne Williams
Harcourt
Based on the author's award-winning poetry, the book draws on her experiences as a child in a migrant, farm-working family.

PHONICS

These books give life to letters and language sounds for fun phonics practice.

ABRAMS ABC'S: EGYPTIAN ART FROM THE BROOKLYN MUSEUM • THE MUSEUM OF MODERN ART, NEW YORK • THE NATIONAL AIR AND SPACE MUSEUM
Abrams
Learn the ABC's with objects from the world's finest museum collections. Collect all the alphabet books in this beautifully presented series.

ACTION ALPHABET
by Marty Neumeir and Byron Glaser
Greenwillow
*Letters come to life as **c** cracks, **r** rains, and **j** jumps!*

ALISON'S ZINNIA
by Anita Lobel
Greenwillow
One flower leads to another in this imaginative exploration of flowers for each letter of the alphabet.

ALPHABATICS
by Suse MacDonald
Bradbury
*Watch **S** transform into a swan and **I** become an insect. Playful associations between the way a letter is formed and the sound it represents.*

ANDY: THAT'S MY NAME
by Tomie DePaola
Prentice
Andy and his friends practice spelling patterns by transforming the letters in Andy's name.

ANIMAL ALPHABET
by Bert Kitchen
Dial
Each letter is elegantly intertwined with a matching animal.

ANIMALIA
by Graema Base
Abrams
Stunning images of a fantastic animal world illustrate alliterations of equal intensity.

ANNO'S ALPHABET: AN ADVENTURE IN IMAGINATION
by Mitsumasa Anno
Crowell
Capital letters in 3-D are illustrated imaginatively along with corresponding pictures.

BRIAN WILDSMITH'S ABC
by Brian Wildsmith
Watts
This award-winning alphabet book uses uniquely drawn everyday objects to illustrate the letter sounds.

CRASH! BANG! BOOM! • GOBBLE, GROWL, GRUNT
by Peter Spier
Doubleday
Entire books of sounds, categorized for a noise-maker's delight!

DR. SEUSS' ABC
by Dr. Seuss
Random House
Have great fun with the alphabet and rhyming language as only Dr. Seuss knows how!

EATING THE ALPHABET
by Lois Ehlert
Harcourt
Brilliant collages introduce readers to a delectable assortment of fruits and vegetables from apples to zucchini.

FROM ALBATROSS TO ZOO: AN ALPHABET BOOK IN FIVE LANGUAGES
by Patricia Borlenchi
Scholastic
Zany animals teach you their names in five different languages.

THE ICKY BUG ALPHABET BOOK
by Jerry Pallotta
Charlesbridge
The many titles in this beautifully illustrated series help children uncover the wonders of nature as they practice letter sounds.

JEN THE HEN • MIG THE PIG • PAT THE CAT • TOG THE DOG
by Colin and Jaqui Hawkins
Putnam
Silly animals teach short vowel words in these cleverly designed books.

WHAT'S INSIDE: THE ALPHABET BOOK
by Satoshi Kitamura
Farrar, Straus, and Giroux
*Many offbeat alphabet surprises: Guess what jumps out of the **c** garbage can or the **m** toothpaste tube.*

THE Z WAS ZAPPED: A PLAY IN TWENTY-SIX ACTS
by Chris Van Allsburg
Houghton Mifflin
This master artist and storyteller creates a ridiculously tragic play with letters of the alphabet as victims.

NONFICTION

Build on children's interest in their world and extend the discoveries they are making with nonfiction books.

ANIMAL ARK BOOKS: COLORFUL • FEATHERY • FURRY • PRICKLY • SCALY •SPOTTY • STRIPY • WRINKLY
by Angela Wilkes
Dorling Kindersley
Each tiny take-along book features a particular category of animal.

ANIMALS SLEEPING • WHOSE BABY? • WHOSE FOOTPRINTS?
by Masayuki Yabuuchi
Putnam
Simple text and elegant paintings introduce your child to nature.

ANTARCTICA • RAIN FOREST
by Helen Cowcher
Farrer, Straus, and Giroux; Scholastic
Magnificent illustrations and rich text acquaint children with these fascinating regions.

BREAD, BREAD, BREAD • HATS, HATS, HATS • ON THE GO
by Ann Morris
Morrow; Scholastic
Ken Heyman's full-color, candid photos provide a rich view of everyday life around the world by focusing on a particular theme.

A CACHE OF JEWELS • KITES SAIL HIGH • MANY LUSCIOUS LOLLIPOPS • UP, UP AND AWAY
by Ruth Heller
Putnam; Scholastic
A colorful exploration of parts of speech and types of words.

CHICKENS AREN'T THE ONLY ONES • PLANTS THAT NEVER BLOOM
by Ruth Heller
Putnam; Scholastic
Unusual phenomena of nature presented through brilliant illustrations and verse. More books in the series.

EYE OPENERS: DINOSAURS • TRUCKS • JUNGLE ANIMALS
Dorling Kindersley
Simple text and full-color photos satisfy the curious who want to know more about the many topics in this series. Something for every interest from kiwis to racing cars to panthers.

FIRST DISCOVERY BOOKS: COLORS • FRUIT • THE WEATHER
by Pascale de Bourgoing
Scholastic
Young explorers can make scientific discoveries by simply turning the transparent pages of these clever books. Many additional titles.

**THE FIVE SENSES • THE FOUR ELEMENTS •
LET'S DISCOVER**
by Maria Rius and J. M. Parramon
Barron's
*Beautiful watercolor illustrations and simple text inspire young
children to learn about their world. Also available in Spanish.*

IF YOU LOOK AROUND YOU
by Fulvio Testa
Dial
An exquisite study of geometry and visual perception.

**I LOVE MY DADDY BECAUSE • I LOVE MY MOMMY
BECAUSE**
by Laurel Porter-Gaylord
Dutton
*Simple text and warm illustrations teach children about
animals and their offspring.*

IN MY GARDEN • IN THE POND • IN THE WOODS
by Ermano Cristini and Luigi Puricelli
Picture Book Studio; Scholastic
*Wordless panoramas of plant and animal life unfold in these
three rich habitats.*

**LET'S EXPLORE SCIENCE SERIES:
MAKE IT BALANCE • MAKE A CHANGE •
ME AND MY BABY • MAKE IT GO**
by David Evans and Claudette Williams
Dorling Kindersley
*Young readers investigate through hands-on experiments.
Easy-to-read text and full-color photos show them how.*

**LET'S-READ-AND-FIND-OUT SCIENCE BOOKS:
DIGGING UP DINOSAUR BONES • GERMS MAKE
ME SICK • WHAT WILL THE WEATHER BE?**
Harper
*The many titles in this series present information in
a fascinating way that appeals to young readers.*

**MACHINES • MY BARBER • MY DOCTOR •
THRUWAY • THE SUPERMARKET**
by Anne and Harlow Rockwell
Macmillan
*Together and separately, these authors have created many
beautiful books for young children. Their boldly illustrated
concept books demystify the adult world.*

**MY FIRST BOOKS:
ACTIVITY • NATURE • SCIENCE • TIME**
Dorling Kindersley
*Life-size activity guides brimming with clear step-by-step
photographs. They are irresistible for anyone who loves
exploring and making things. Many more topics available.*

ON THE DAY YOU WERE BORN
by Debra Fraser
Harcourt
Experience the natural forces at work on that very special day.

PLANTING A RAINBOW • RED LEAF, YELLOW LEAF
by Lois Ehlert
Harcourt
*Vibrant collages tell the story of a colorful bouquet from seed
to flower. The next book uses collage to tell of the wondrous
growth of a maple tree through the eyes of the child who
planted it.*

**READ AND WONDER: ALL PIGS ARE BEAUTIFUL •
A PIECE OF STRING IS A WONDERFUL THING •
THINK OF A BEAVER •THINK OF AN EEL**
Candlewick Press
*Poetic nonfiction would best describe these lovely picture books
filled with stories, poems, facts, ideas, and artwork all centering
around a fascinating topic.*

**THE SCIENCE BOOK OF: AIR • COLOR • LIGHT •
WATER • ELECTRICITY**
Harcourt
*Simple to follow experiments with step-by-step photographs
teach basic scientific principles to young learners.*

SEE HOW THEY GROW: DUCK • FROG • KITTEN
Dutton
*Informative photographs chart the stages of a young animal's
growth.*

**SIERRA CLUB'S GROWING UP BOOKS:
OTTER SWIMS • PANDA CLIMBS • TIGER RUNS**
by Derek Hall
Knopf
Learn about young animals by joining them on their adventures.

**STARTING OUT BOOKS: MY NEW SCHOOL •
MY BABY BROTHER •OUR NEW KITTEN**
by Harriet Haines
Dorling Kindersley
*Unique photographic storybooks take the fear out
of new experiences.*

**STARTING SCIENCE: ANIMALS • FOOD •
SOUND AND MUSIC**
by Kay Davies and Wendy Oldfield
Steck-Vaughn
*Full-color photographs give young explorers the steps
they need for hands-on experimentation.*

THIS IS MY HOUSE
by Arthur Durros
Scholastic
*Journey around the world, exploring the similarities
and differences of homes.*

WHAT'S INSIDE: TOYS • MY BODY • INSECTS
Dorling Kindersley
*Detailed photographs and drawings take you inside everything
from a Teddy bear to a space suit. There are many more titles in
the series.*

**WHO CHANGES INTO WHAT? • WHO EATS WHAT? •
WHO LIVES HERE? • WHO IS IN THE WATER?**
by Ron and Atie van der Meer
Price Stern Sloan
*Guess the answer to science questions, then see if you're right
by pulling a tab.*

MAGAZINES

What fun to receive a readable monthly magazine specially
addressed to your child!

CHICKADEE
Young Naturalist Foundation
255 Great Arrow Avenue
Buffalo, NY 14207
56 The Esplanade, Suite 306
Toronto, Ontario M5E 1A7 Canada
*A science magazine filled with hands-on activities
for the young naturalist.*

HUMPTY DUMPTY • TURTLE
P.O. Box 7134
Red Oak, IA
The first activity magazine is recommended for ages 4-6. The second is for ages 2-5.

LADYBUG
315 5th Street
Peru, IL 61354
Jam-packed with quality language activities for the young.

LET'S FIND OUT • MY FIRST MAGAZINE
Scholastic
2931 E. McCarty Street
Jefferson City, MO 65101
Stories and skill activities for kindergartners in the first listing and preschoolers in the second.

MICKEY MOUSE MAGAZINE
P.O. Box 10598
Des Moines, IA 50340
Activities for Disney fans of all ages.

SESAME STREET
Children's Television Workshop
P.O. Box 52000
Boulder, CO 80321-2000
Basic concepts, reading, writing, math readiness, Spanish, and signing all taught by Big Bird and company. Includes parents' guide.

YOUR BIG BACKYARD
National Wildlife Federation
1412 16th Street, NW
Washington, DC 20036-9967
An appreciation for wildlife and the environment is learned along with science facts and reading skills. Beautifully photographed and illustrated in full color. Includes parents' guide.

WRITING

These resources inspire enthusiasm for writing.

THE BOOKERY
6899 Riata Drive
Redding, CA 96002
*Order everything you need to create a beautiful hand-bound volume: **Hey Look, I Made a Book** by Betty Doty and Rebecca Meredith, plus supplies.*

FREE STUFF FOR KIDS
Meadowbrook Press
A wonderful resource for proving that writing is vital communication. Hundreds of places children can write and receive back the "safe, fun, and informative things kids like."

INKADINKADO
76 South Street
Boston, MA 02111
Send for a stamp-maniac's dream catalog. Every kind of stamp is available, from ones that roll out your child's name to custom stamps of his own design.

QUILL OFFICE PRODUCTS
100 Schelter Road
Lincolnshire, IL 60069-9972
This is the ultimate source for markers, paper, business forms, and so on at discount prices, by mail. Some items are only sold in quantity, but small orders are also welcome.

YOU BE THE AUTHOR
by Jill Hauser
Good Apple, Inc.
Twenty exciting mini books for young writers to assemble and author.

AUDIO RECORDINGS

Titles of audio recordings of children's stories are too numerous to mention. Look for display racks in children's book and music stores. Book clubs often offer cassettes to accompany their titles. What follows are sources for audio recordings of favorite songs and stories.

ALCAZAR
P.O. Box 429
Waterbury, VT 05676-0429
800-541-9904
*Request their **Kiddy Cat** (short for catalog) listing 200 of their best of the over 2000 children's story and music cassettes, CDs, and videos that they carry.*

CAEDMON
HarperCollins
Keystone Industrial Park
Scranton, PA 18512-4621
800-331-3761
*Caedmon has received numerous awards for their quality recordings of children's literature. Works are either read by the author or outstanding actors. **Caedmon for Kids** is a series of favorite paperbacks and accompanying musical story cassettes.*

KIDS SONGS
Klutz Press
2121 Staunton Court
Palo Alto, CA 94306
A spirited music collection that's sure to delight. Each cassette comes with a colorful industrial strength songbook that invites young reader/singers to follow along with the words, again and again.

LISTENING LIBRARY
1 Park Avenue
Old Greenwich, CT O6870
800-243-4504
Popular books read by authors or top narrators. Productions are unabridged. A wide range of cassettes appeal to ages four through adult. Listening Library is also a source for BookMates, adorable puppet and stuffed animal book characters.

MUSIC FOR LITTLE PEOPLE
Box 1460
Redway, CA 95560
800-727-2233
A joyous collection of quality audio, video, musical instruments, and more available by mail.

RABBIT EARS
131 Rowayton Avenue
Rowayton, CT 06853
Listening Library
800-243-4504
A beautiful, award-winning collection of legends, classic, international and biblical tales. Each story is available on cassette, CD, or video. Narrators are celebrity actors. Notable artist and composers add their talents for a very special interpretation of these favorite stories.

SCHOLASTIC
P.O. Box 7502
Jefferson City MO 65102-9968
800-325-6149
Cassettes are available for many of their book club titles. Order through your child's school or from your own book and cassette ordering group.

WEE SING BOOKS AND TAPES
Price Stern Sloan
P.O. Box 64575
Los Angeles, CA 90064
800-421-0892
Every possible collection of classic songs: campfire, lullaby, holiday, and so on. If you've ever wanted to sing a song to your child from your childhood but forgot the words, here they are.

COMPUTER SOFTWARE

Unlike a book, you can't thumb through software when you pick it off the shelf. Software availability changes continually with new products coming out on the market and old products being updated. Check the packaging for reviews and awards, descriptions of the activities, and photographs of the program's screens. Try to buy software from a store or mail-order house that will give you a money-back guarantee. What follows is a brief list of some of the many quality programs available. Also included are parent guides to software.

INTERACTIVE SOFTWARE

BAILEY'S BOOK HOUSE
Edmark
Let Bailey help your child create stories and messages, recognize words, practice rhyme, and more. Colorful animation and a lifelike voice inspire skill practice.

KID WORKS 2
Davidson
Award-winning children's word processing and illustration program. Activities are all wonderfully open-ended. The stories children create can be printed and even read aloud by the computer.

THE PLAYROOM
Broderbund
Award winning software offers a wide variety of easy-to-control activities. "ABC" lets children watch a street scene of letters magically become the objects they stand for.

READER RABBIT 1 AND 2 • READY FOR LETTERS
Learning Company
Award-winning programs develop a variety of skills such as matching and sorting, letter sound identification, and word building. Reader Rabbit is the guide in various fantasy settings.

CD-ROM STORYBOOKS

KIDS CAN READ • LITTLE KIDS CAN READ
Discis
Actual text and illustrations from favorite children's stories are enlivened with real voices, music, and sound effects. Text is highlighted as it is read. Clicked-on words are pronounced.

LIVING BOOKS: ARTHUR'S TEACHER TROUBLE • JUST GRANDMA AND ME
Broderbund
Award-winning software wherein children can opt to hear the story read aloud, even in several languages, while corresponding sections of the text are highlighted. By clicking on hotspots on the screen children can trigger amusing animation sequences.

SOFTWARE GUIDES

HIGH/ SCOPE BUYER'S GUIDE TO CHILDREN'S SOFTWARE: ANNUAL SURVEY OF COMPUTER PROGRAMS FOR CHILDREN AGES 3 TO 7
by Warren Buckleitner
High/Scope Educational Research Foundation
This definitive guide sets out tough criteria, then evaluates and gives a number ranking to more than 500 programs for young children, yearly. Their award-winners are sure bets.

KIDS AND COMPUTERS: A PARENT'S HANDBOOK
by Judy Salpeter
SAMS
A thorough look at computer use by children. Offers guidance in hardware and software selection. Filled with practical advise for helping children become computer-literate.

THE LEARNING CUBE
3 Pine Ridge Way
Mill Valley, CA 94941
800-733-6733
The catalog lists over 150 highly acclaimed software products for children, including hard-to-find programs. Reviews and ratings are given along with program descriptions. Programs must meet the Cube's high standards for educational value, ease of use, and child appeal in order to be stocked.

PARENT/TEACHER RESOURCES

RESEARCH

Reading is perhaps the most researched field of education. These resources put the studies in perspective and offer research-based recommendations for instruction.

BECOMING A NATION OF READERS: REPORT OF THE COMMISSION ON READING
National Institute of Education
This landmark report informs you of what to expect from the reading program your child will encounter in school. It identifies the practices of the best teachers in the best schools and suggests they be introduced everywhere.

BEGINNING TO READ: THINKING AND LEARNING ABOUT PRINT
by Marilyn Adams
Center for the Study of Reading
A concise and definitive review of the vast body of research regarding the beginning stages of learning to read.

JOURNAL OF READING
International Reading Association
Monthly publication directed to educators. Cutting-edge analysis of the research. Helps educators put theory into practice.

Remember, the most effective way to continue reading success is to provide books just too good to put down, both for reading aloud and independent reading. The following are resource listings of these fine books.

CHILDREN'S BOOKS: AWARDS AND PRIZES
The Children's Book Council
A compilation of children's books honored throughout the world. A non-evaluative listing, revised biennially. Look for it in the reference section of your library.

CHILDREN'S CHOICE
International Reading Association
A yearly listing of newly published books selected by young readers themselves.

CHOOSING BOOKS FOR KIDS: HOW TO CHOOSE THE RIGHT BOOK FOR THE RIGHT CHILD AT THE RIGHT TIME
by Joanne Oppenheim et al.
Ballantine
Reviews 1,500 titles from baby's first books to those for teens. Helps you match book selection to your child's development.

FOR LOVE OF READING
by Masha Rudman and Anna Pearce
Consumer Reports Books
Offers specific ideas and activities for making the most of specially selected books for each stage of your child's development.

MICHELE LANDSBERG'S GUIDE TO CHILDREN'S BOOKS
by Michele Landsberg
Penguin (Canada)
This authoritative guide sensitively discusses hundreds of books for all ages. Includes excellent Canadian children's books.

NEW YORK TIMES GUIDE TO THE BEST BOOKS FOR CHILDREN
by Eden Ross Lipson
Times Books
*The children's book editor for the **New York Times** recommends nearly 1,000 books in this well-organized and indexed guide.*

THE READ-ALOUD HANDBOOK
by Jim Trelease
Penguin
This handbook has quickly become the bible of read-aloud books. But don't only read these great books aloud; the same reasons they were chosen for reading aloud make them excellent choices for independent reading.

RECOMMENDED READINGS IN LITERATURE
California State Department of Education
P.O. Box 271
Sacramento, CA 95802-0271
Recommended reading for kindergarten through grade 8. Indicates appropriate grade span for over 1,000 works.

The following are organizations devoted to literacy and/or children's issues.

AMERICAN LIBRARY ASSOCIATION
50 East Huron Street
Chicago, IL 60611
Committed to library service as a way to enhance learning and insure access to information for all. Request a catalog of literacy promotional material.

CHILDREN'S BOOK COUNCIL
67 Irving Place
New York, NY 10003
A nonprofit association of children's trade book publishers promoting international literacy through a variety of projects. Request their catalog of literacy-promoting graphics and other materials.

INTERNATIONAL READING ASSOCIATION
800 Barksdale Road,
P.O. Box 8139
Newark, DE 19714-8139
*Publishers of **The Reading Teacher, The Journal of Reading, Reading Research Quarterly, Lectura Y Vida, Children's Choice,** and a variety of books and brochures. Sponsors of conferences promoting quality literacy instruction.*

NATIONAL ASSOCIATION FOR THE EDUCATION OF YOUNG CHILDREN
1834 Connecticut Avenue, NW.
Washington, DC 20009-5786
*Committed to fostering the development of children through age eight. Publishers of the journal, **Young Children** and numerous other publications. Sponsors of **Week of the Young Child** and conferences.*

PARENTS' CHOICE FOUNDATION
Box 185
Waburn, MA 02168
*Sponsors of a variety of projects related to the evaluation of children's media. They publish **Parents' Choice**, "the only nonprofit consumer guide to children's books, toys, video, audio, computer programs, television, magazine and rock 'n' roll." Their awards issue contains a gold mine of exceptional products.*

READING IS FUNDAMENTAL
600 Maryland Avenue, SW, Suite 600
Washington, D.C. 20024
Committed to inspiring children to read. They publish numerous parent guide brochures and booklets. Sponsors of a variety of literacy-promoting projects and events.

Growing Up Reading for Early Childhood Education Programs

THE LITERACY-RICH CLASSROOM

Imagine this classroom: A child snuggles up to a stuffed rabbit and retells, *Goodnight Moon*. Two other children listen intently to a story through earphones. Several children enthusiastically write, cut, draw, and paste at a low table brimming with writing and art supplies. A small group is using puppets to dramatize *Three Billy Goats Gruff*. Several children mix play dough with their teacher as they all refer to a poster-sized recipe. One youngster distributes "mail" into the cubbies of her classmates. Those building with blocks add road signs to their city. Children refer to magazines in the playhouse. The classroom is bursting with print. Cubbies are labeled with children's names. The hatching of a new chick is celebrated with posters illustrating and describing the daily events. Word mobiles display thematic vocabulary. Procedures, songs, and stories are written on large posters that decorate the classroom along with children's own writing and drawing.

The message children get in this classroom is clear — written language is an essential and enjoyable part of life. How the teacher structures the classroom environment, the kinds of activities she offers, and the learning climate she creates, will determine what children learn about print.

STRUCTURING THE ENVIRONMENT

We know children learn from interacting with their environment, so lets give them an environment rich with print. The physical space of the classroom can be structured purposefully to promote literacy. Literacy becomes a natural and integral part of the operation of the classroom.

Start by creating a "literacy hub" that is the core of the classroom. The hub consists of these centers: a library, writing center, and an oral language center. The size and location of each center within the Literacy Hub will depend on your space constraints. Involve the children in creating each center. They are more likely to use these areas if they've made a personal investment in the center's creation. Centers should look inviting with attractive posters and friendly furniture.

Centers should grow and change with children's needs and interests. Start new centers with a minimum of supplies and materials. Continually add new items throughout the year. Children will make the best use of materials you have demonstrated and introduced. For example, add a new library book each time you read one aloud. Warm children up to a stock of public library books that will be in the classroom library for the next few weeks. After telling a flannel board story, make the equipment available in the Oral Language Center. Offer book-making supplies after children have made books with teacher direction. Show off some new office forms or unusual paper you were able to acquire. Remove materials children are not using and reintroduce them later in the year. Recirculating materials keeps the Literacy Hub vital and exciting. Continually visit the centers to model their importance. Volunteers and aides can be available in the centers to read books aloud, take story dictation, or encourage dramatic play. Offer literacy-building materials for a wide range of abilities. Not all children will make full use of the materials, but each will grow from interacting in her own way with books, audio recordings, tactile letters, and so on.

THE LIBRARY

Design a library where children will read.

- Provide space for several children. A carpet or a few cushions invite a small group of children to share books.
- Provide a place for privacy. A bean bag chair or rocking chair set apart with a bookcase invites independent reading.
- Store most books on shelves with spines facing out. Include books, magazines, and catalogs for a wide range of interests and abilities. Include books created by individual children, the teacher, and the entire classroom.
- Also use a bookshelf that displays special books with the front cover facing out. Or, use individual book racks set on shelf tops to display special books. These might be books the children have heard read aloud or those pertaining to a particular theme the children are studying.
- Provide duplicate copies of popular books to encourage children to read with a friend.
- If possible, categorize the books by topic, using different colored tape or stickers on the book's spine for each topic. For example, animal books might be labeled red or weather books, green.
- Recirculate books to maintain interest. Replace old books with new books you've read aloud. Reintroduce the old books later in the year.
- Make available stuffed animals resembling storybook characters such as a red dog for Clifford or a monkey for Curious George. (Order Bookmate stuffed storybook characters and puppets from Listening Library, 800-243-4504.)
- Use a bulletin board or wall to display commercial, teacher-made, or child-made posters celebrating the joy of reading. Display children's art depicting favorite storybook characters or scenes.

THE WRITING CENTER

Create an area where all forms of writing thrive.

- Provide chairs and a low table large enough for several writers to work simultaneously.
- Use shallow boxes to organize and store a vast array of writing and simple art supplies: pencils, ball-point pens, felt markers, colored pencils, blank paper, lined paper, business forms, stationery, envelopes, stamps, staplers, tape, hole punch, scissors, paste, rubber stamps and stamps pads, magazines, and newspapers.
- Set aside some materials specifically for book making.
- Encourage all forms of writing: scribbles, drawings, pretend writing, cutting and pasting magazine words and pictures.
- Use a bulletin board or wall to display children's writing and art work.
- Post an alphabet chart for easy reference.
- Make tactile letters and alphabet puzzles available for manipulation.
- Provide a chalk or marker board message center for teacher and child messages.
- If possible, provide a typewriter or computer.
- Make a mailbox where writers may leave mail and messages addressed to other classmates.
- Consider placing the art center near the writing center to encourage multi-media work. Welcome combination painted, drawn, taped, and written masterpieces.

ORAL LANGUAGE CENTER

Create an area that supports story-talk and other oral language.

- Provide a flannel board with felt pieces that children can manipulate to retell a familiar tale.
- Collect a variety of puppets and old costumes for dramatizing stories.
- If possible, make a simple stage for puppet shows and one for plays.
- Provide a sturdy tape recorder for recording children's storytelling.
- Set up a playback unit and earphones for listening to favorite stories.

THROUGHOUT THE CLASSROOM

Fill the classroom environment with functional print.

- Label all cubbies, supplies, and shelves. If you use symbols or pictures as labels, add words as well.
- Display a calendar, thermometer, and clock for reading.
- Post charts listing or describing routines, procedures, attendance, helpers.
- Post words and illustrations to favorite songs.
- Hang word mobiles of thematic vocabulary over areas where those words are used. Add pictures to add meaning.
- Display stories told by the class and recorded by the teacher.
- Record, chart, and post observations in the science center.
- Post recipes in the cooking center.
- Include print props appropriate to the current theme in the dramatic play area.

LITERACY–PROMOTING ACTIVITIES

ADAPTING *GROWING UP READING* ACTIVITIES TO GROUPS

You can bring any activity suggested at the end of each chapter in this book into the classroom. Place all materials required for a particular activity on a tray or within a shallow box. Demonstrate the activity to a small group of children, inviting their participation. Then make the activity available for children to try on their own. Place activity trays on low shelves children can easily access. Have children take the chosen activity to a work table to try independently or with a friend. Each time you demonstrate an activity, make it available to the children as described above. Soon your shelves will be brimming with a variety of literacy-building activities from which children can choose.

On the Go activities are a perfect way to start or end group time. Children benefit greatly from brainstorming answers and ideas in a group. One child's response inspires another child.

Please note that this is a general discussion about early childhood education programs. Whether you direct a child care center, a pre-school, or a first grade class, will determine the kinds of learning activities you select. Follow the same *Guidelines for Success* (see Introduction) offered to parents to determine the appropriateness of activities when selecting them for your group.

SENSORY EXPLORATION AND CONCEPT BUILDING

Sensory exploration and concept building are the core of early childhood education programs. The activities described in chapter 2 are typical program activities. Remember, in order to prepare children for reading and writing, add plenty of language to their experiences. Encourage children to talk about their discoveries. Extend their language as you respond. Act as a scribe for class poster-sized stories or individual stories about class events and experiences. Display and use special vocabulary words related to themes you are exploring.

CHANTS, SONGS, AND RHYMES

Chants, songs, and rhymes are the music of early childhood education programs. Clearly print out the words to favorites on poster-sized paper. Line up repeating phrases so children get a visual sense of the song's structure. Sketch illustrations to add meaning. At group time, point to the words as the children sing along. Compose original versions to favorite songs. Lyrics can reflect the theme you are studying.

For children ready to delve deeper into print, pass out separate sentences from the song, printed on long strips of paper. Have pairs of children stand and hold up their strip as it is sung. Laying the poster on a table, invite a small group to match their sentence strips with the sentences on the poster.

DRAMATIC PLAY

The dramatic play center can be a stage for oral language practice and experimentation with print. The kinds of props offered guide the children in their play. Add strips of cloth to the doctor's kit, and suddenly patients will be bandaged. Add a toy phone, and appointments will be arranged. Children discover how useful these tools are by trying them out while they play.

They can also discover how useful, and powerful, reading and writing are if "print props" are made available for exploration. After all, print is a vital part of the adult-world on which their play is based. Offer magazines while children play doctor's office and patients will "read" in the waiting room. Give the doctor a clipboard, paper, and pencil, and she'll "write" out a medical history. During dramatic play, encourage children to write on blank forms and to read instructions and signs in their own way. Unless children see print as crucial to reaching their goals, they won't be interested in learning to read or write.

Change the theme of the center to match themes you are studying. For example, if your theme is transportation, the center might become an airplane or travel agency. A food theme might inspire a bakery, grocery store, or fast-food restaurant. Here are some dramatic play center themes and corresponding print props:

- **Travel agency, airport, bus, or train station:** Tickets, schedules, travel brochures and guides, maps, postcards, travel posters, play money, luggage tags, magazines, and books.
- **Medical clinic, dentist office, optometrist, veteri-nary hospital:** Medical history and diagnosis forms, eye chart, prescriptions, bills, health care brochures, clipboard, magazines, books, appointment cards, and a calendar.
- **Museum, art gallery:** Brochures, descriptive labels for pieces, price tags, art and object books, tickets.
- **Market, bakery, store:** Signs labeling items for sale, empty product containers, advertisements, coupons, receipts, promotional signs, bags displaying store's logo, play money.

- **Theater, movie house, television studio:** Tickets, play money, programs, promotional posters, programs, scripts, entrance/exit signs.
- **Office, post office, bank:** Business forms and cards, rubber stamps, stamp pads, envelopes, stamps, play money, notebooks, clipboards, filing supplies, open/closed signs, withdrawal/deposit slips.
- **Restaurant, fast-food shop:** Menus, menu board, recipe books, order pads, money, promotional signs, receipts.

Children must understand the *reasons* for written language to gain control over it and put it to use. Adding print props to their dramatic play is an easy and natural way for them to experience these reasons.

SHARING BOOKS

Reading aloud at least one book should be part of the daily routine. The suggestions for making the most of read-aloud time given in chapter 4 can also be applied to groups. Children benefit from hearing about each other's experiences that pertain to the book as you warm them up to the story or topic. As well as making their own predictions, group reading allows them to react to each other's predictions. Large, poster-sized "big books" of favorite picture books allow every child to comfortably see the illustrations and text. (Big books are available from Scholastic, 800-325-6149.)

After the story is read, you may wish to extend the children's understanding and enjoyment through art, drama, music, or writing. See *Folk Tale Fun* on page 58 for specific activities. Children's understanding and enjoyment of nonfiction can be extended with similar activities. For example, after reading a book about beavers, children can pretend they are beavers and dramatize the building of their lodge. They can draw pictures of beavers caring for their young or looking for food. They can write a class story telling all they know about beavers.

Invite special classroom visitors, parents, or school staff to read aloud to the class. Children can write invitations and thank you notes to the guests. The guest's arrival proves the power of print as a communication media along with bringing the enjoyment of a good story to the children. Guests should bring a picture book that is important to them and share the reason with the children. The story can be tape recorded onto an anthology tape for later enjoyment in the listening area (see *Audio Recordings, Activities*, page 58). Hearing books read aloud by guest readers assures children that the joy of reading extends beyond their classroom walls.

SPECIAL WORDS

Offer children a way to keep the words they request. Print words on index cards with a hole punched in the corner. Cards for individuals may be ringed together with the child's name on the top card. Encourage children to share their word bundles at home. They may wish to illustrate their cards to add meaning to them. Cards may be kept in desks or cubbies. More elaborate ways to keep track of words would be to list them in word books or file them into alphabetized or topic-categorized recipe boxes.

Have a Special Word Celebration where each child wears a special word on a string around her neck. The room will buzz with "What does that say?" as children share their words.

WRITING

In addition to setting up a writing center, let writing thrive as part of the natural functioning of the classroom. Here are some ways:

- Let children catch you in the act of writing.
- Involve children in the making of procedure, helper, and attendance charts; special notices and warning signs; lists of supplies, ingredients, and children.
- Treat children as the true readers and writers they are by inviting them to write and then read their work in their own way.
- Encourage children to write their names on their art and other work, again in their own way.
- Encourage writing in children's play.
- Invite children to write, "about anything you like."
- Encourage all forms of writing as acceptable and real. "Write in your own way. It doesn't have to look like my writing." The more accepting you are as teacher and model, the more writing will flow.
- Encourage all forms of writing by displaying every child's work.
- Encourage children to share their writing with each other.
- Send work home for children to share with parents.
- Let parents know why all forms of writing are acceptable.
- Let children write invitations and thank you notes to special visitors.
- Let children experience writing as communication by setting up a classroom postal service. Help children write their friend's name on their message. Let a child who can read the names deliver the messages, or let children simply place messages in each other's cubbies.

BOOK MAKING

Start out with a discussion at group time about the topic of the book to be made. For example, with *I Love*, talk with the children about what they love. List their ideas on the blackboard. Have children repeat the complete sentence with you as they offer their suggestions: "Rabbits. I love rabbits. Cookies. I love cookies. The lake. I love the lake." Photocopy a class set of *I Love* book sheets from appendix B. Work with small groups of interested children assembling, writing, and illustrating the books. Children may want you to write their words or they may prefer their own writing. Have children share finished books in the library.

The fastest way to produce library books children love to read is to create classroom books. Each child makes one page. Give each child an 8 1/2" x 11" sheet of paper. Change the structure of *I love* ———, to ——— loves ———. At the top of the sheet write or have the children write their sentence, *Jane loves clay* or *Matt loves frogs*. Have children illustrate their sentence. Now bind all pages into a single book (see *Binding*, page 102). Use stiff laminated paper for the cover. Classroom books are sure favorites that will be read again and again. Classroom books can be written on any topic. (See *What's the Big Idea*, page 98.)

No classroom should be without a "classroom scrapbook" similar to the "Me" Scrapbook described on page 58. Fill the pages with captioned photos of the children, children's accounts and pictures of special events, lyrics to favorite songs, souvenirs from outings and special guests, and anything that says, "This is what we are all about." Have children design the cover and give the book a special name. Laminate the pages as they are completed, since this volume will be a very popular reading choice.

BUILD A COMMUNITY OF COOPERATIVE LEARNERS

Perhaps the most important way to positively influence literacy learning is to create a classroom community where everyone, their ideas, and their work, are accepted and welcome — where learning is a joyful process. A classroom can be a place where cooperative learning thrives. Children learn much from interacting with each other: They can brainstorm ideas, model skills, be reading and writing buddies, engage in pretend play, and produce plays, to name just a few of the many activities in which two or more can be better than one. How you as teacher/model design the classroom and respond to the children greatly influence how much cooperation and joyful learning take place. Here are some suggestions:

• Model patience, courtesy, and respect.
• Be calm and maintain a sense of humor.
• Be a good listener.
• Focus on children's strengths instead of weaknesses; what is right instead of what is wrong.
• Offer children real choices.
• Offer learning activities that genuinely interest the children.
• Create a nonthreatening environment where risk-taking and experimentation are encouraged.
• Structure the classroom so children can work independently or cooperatively.
• Acknowledge the knowledge children bring with them to the classroom.
• Elicit their ideas and opinions on classroom issues that concern them.
• Involve children in classroom management such as rule making and center care.
• Be enthusiastic about the children and their work.
• Instill the self-image in each child that she is a reader and a writer.
• Have the expectation that every child will learn.

Activity Materials

ACTIVITY MATERIALS

 PREPARING THE MATERIALS

Prepare the materials provided for selected activities throughout the book. Here's how:

1. Photocopy the page. You may prefer to use heavy stock. Photocopy on both sides (back-to-back) only where indicated.

2. Carefully cut along all dashed lines.

3. Stack the cards you've cut out with the title card on top. Use a paper clip or resealable baggie to group cards together. Note that some of the activity sheets are ready to use without cutting.

 USING THE MATERIALS

Activity cards vary in size. Manipulating the smaller cards helps develop the fine muscle control your child needs for writing. The variety of print sizes and styles acquaints him with print that he'll encounter as he becomes a more sophisticated reader. Lower-case letters are emphasized since they appear far more frequently in print.

CONTENTS

Thinking and Comprehension
Environments
Prediction Cards

Language
Real World Reading
Twinkle, Twinkle, Little Star
Old MacDonald

Valuing Reading
I Can Read Books
Love Coupons

Independent Reading
Sentence Springboards
I Love the Mountains
Come to the Circus

Writing
Letter-Sound Cards
Word Construction

FIRST READING BOOKS

 ASSEMBLING THE BOOKS

Assemble the *First Reading Books* from the pages following the activities. Here's how:

1. Photocopy the pages back-to-back as indicated in instructions (or staple back-to-back).

2. Cut each large page along the dashed lines to create the reading book pages. Fold along solid lines.

3. Put the pages you have cut out in order according to the number at the bottom of each page of parent-made book.

4. Bind the book by stapling close to the left edge.

CONTENTS

1, 2!

I Love

Hello

Can

Eat

ENVIRONMENTS

sky

land

water

car

dog

fish

boat

boy

house

starfish

seahorse

rat

tree

seaweed

octopus

butterfly

bee

helicopter

sun

airplane

bat

PREDICTION CARDS

1, 2!

1

1, 2, Buckle my shoe.

3

To assemble, photocopy or staple page 144 back-to-back with page 143.

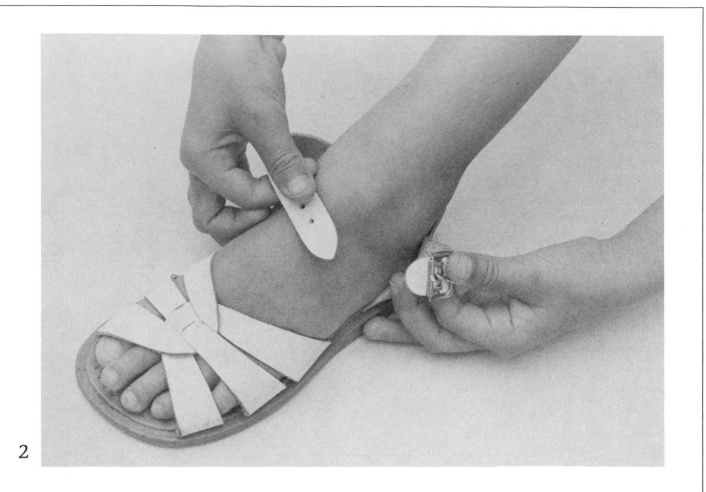

2

4

3, 4, Shut the door.

5

5, 6, Pick up sticks.

7

6

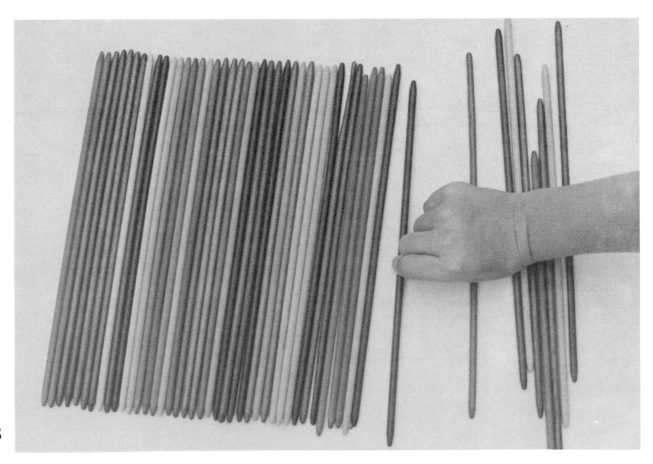

8

7, 8,
Lay them straight.

9

9, 10,
A big fat hen.

11

To assemble, photocopy or staple page 148 back-to-back with page 147.

10

Reader's Review
What did you think of my book?

1, 2 !

12

Welcome
to

Restaurant

Menu

Desserts

_____ $ . . . .

_____ $ . . . .

_____ $ . . . .

Enjoy
your meal.

Come back soon!

To assemble, photocopy or staple page 150 back-to-back with page 149.

Menu

Specials

1. _____ $ _____

2. _____ $ _____

3. _____ $ _____

4. _____ $ _____

Beverages

_____ $ _____

_____ $ _____

_____ $ _____

_____ $ _____

Children's Choice
For children under the age of 12.

_____ $ _____

_____ $ _____

We use only the freshest ingredients.

Our food is carefully prepared for your dining enjoyment.

🍴 Thank You!

Please let us know how you liked your meal.

FOOD **SERVICE**
☐ ☐ EXCELLENT
☐ ☐ GOOD
☐ ☐ FAIR
☐ ☐ POOR

<u>Comments:</u>

_____
_____
_____

Please come again.

Family Health Center

☎ WHILE YOU WERE OUT

To _____

From _____

of _____

Date _____ Time _____

Phone Number _____

Message _____
_____
_____
_____
_____

☐ URGENT ☐ RETURNED YOUR CALL ☐ WILL CALL AGAIN
☐ WANTS TO SEE YOU ☐ REQUESTS CALL BACK ☐ WAS IN

📌 MEMO

Date _____

To _____

From _____

Message _____
_____
_____
_____
_____
_____
_____
_____

To assemble, photocopy or staple page 152 back-to-back with page 151.

Family Health Center

☎ _____ Dr. _____

Patient _____ Date _____

Address _____

℞

Take _____ ☐ teaspoons ☐ tablets

every _____ hours

for _____ days.

Refill • 1 • 2 • 3   Dr. _____
signature

🍴 GUEST CHECK

TABLE NO.	NO. PERSONS	SERVER NO.

QTY.	ITEM	COST

MEMO

Date _____

To _____

From _____

Message _____

_____

_____

_____

_____

_____

☎ WHILE YOU WERE OUT

To _____

From _____

of _____

Date _____ Time _____

Phone Number _____

Message _____

_____

_____

_____

_____

☐ URGENT   ☐ RETURNED YOUR CALL   ☐ WILL CALL AGAIN

☐ WANTS TO SEE YOU   ☐ REQUESTS CALL BACK   ☐ WAS IN

Twinkle, Twinkle, Little Star

Twinkle, twinkle, little star.
How I wonder what you are.

Up above the world so high.
Like a diamond in the sky.

Twinkle, twinkle, little star.
How I wonder what you are.

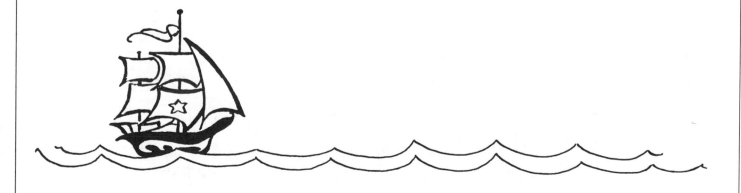

Old MacDonald

Old MacDonald had a farm.

E - I - E - I - O

And on this farm he had a _____.

E - I - E - I - O

With a _____ _____ here.

And a _____ _____ there.

Here a _____. There a _____.

Everywhere a _____ _____.

Old MacDonald had a farm.

E - I - E - I - O

Old MacDonald Word Cards

dog	sheep	snake	brap
r-r-r	ba	s-s-s	nac
r-r-r	ba	s-s-s	nac
r-r-r	ba	s-s-s	nac
r-r-r	ba	s-s-s	nac
r-r-r	ba	s-s-s	nac
r-r-r	ba	s-s-s	nac
r-r-r	ba	s-s-s	nac
r-r-r	ba	s-s-s	nac

Twinkle Sentence Strips

Twinkle, twinkle, little star.

How I wonder what you are.

Up above the world so high.

Like a diamond in the sky.

Twinkle, twinkle, little star.

How I wonder what you are.

I Can Read!

by ....

I can read ....

I can read

2

I can read

4

I can read

5

I can read

7

I can read _____.

6

Reader's Review

What do you think of my book?
What can *you* read?

8

Love Coupon

Please use by _____.

Love Coupon

Please use by _____.

Love Coupon

Please use by _____.

Love Coupon

Please use by _____.

Love Coupon

Please use by _____.

Love Coupon

Please use by _____.

To:_____

From:_____

I will _____

_____

_____

_____

To:_____

From:_____

I will _____

_____

_____

To:_____

From:_____

I will _____

_____

_____

To:_____

From:_____

I will _____

_____

_____

To:_____

From:_____

I will _____

_____

_____

To:_____

From:_____

I will _____

_____

_____

I love

I can

Hi

I Love the Mountains

I love the mountains.
I love the rolling hills.
I love the flowers.
I love the daffodils.
I love the fireside
When all the lights
are low.

Boom de ah duh
Boom de ah duh
Boom de ah duh
Boom de ah duh
Boom, boom, boom

To assemble, photocopy or staple page 164 back-to-back with page 163.

I LOVE THE MOUNTAINS

I love the moun-tains, I love the rol-ling hills,

I love the flow-ers, I love the daf-fo-dils,

I love the fire-side when all the lights are low,

Boom-de-ah-duh, Boom-de-ah-duh, Boom-de-ah-duh, Boom-de-ah-duh

ENDING

Boom, boom, boom

3

2

I love

I love

People love

I Love!

I Love!

by ....

© *date* ....

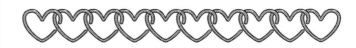

To assemble, photocopy or staple page 166 back-to-back with page 165.

$\textsf{ə} \land \textsf{o} l \text{ I}$.

$\textsf{ə} \land \textsf{o} l \text{ I}$.

About the Book

You'll love reading **I Love!** Discover four of the many things author _____ loves.

About the Author

Author _____ is _____ years old. _____ lives in the city of _____.

Author

a b c

d e f

g h i

j	k	l
m	n	o
p	q	r

s t u

v w x

LETTER-SOUND
CARDS

y z

LETTER-SOUND CARDS

LETTER-SOUND CARDS

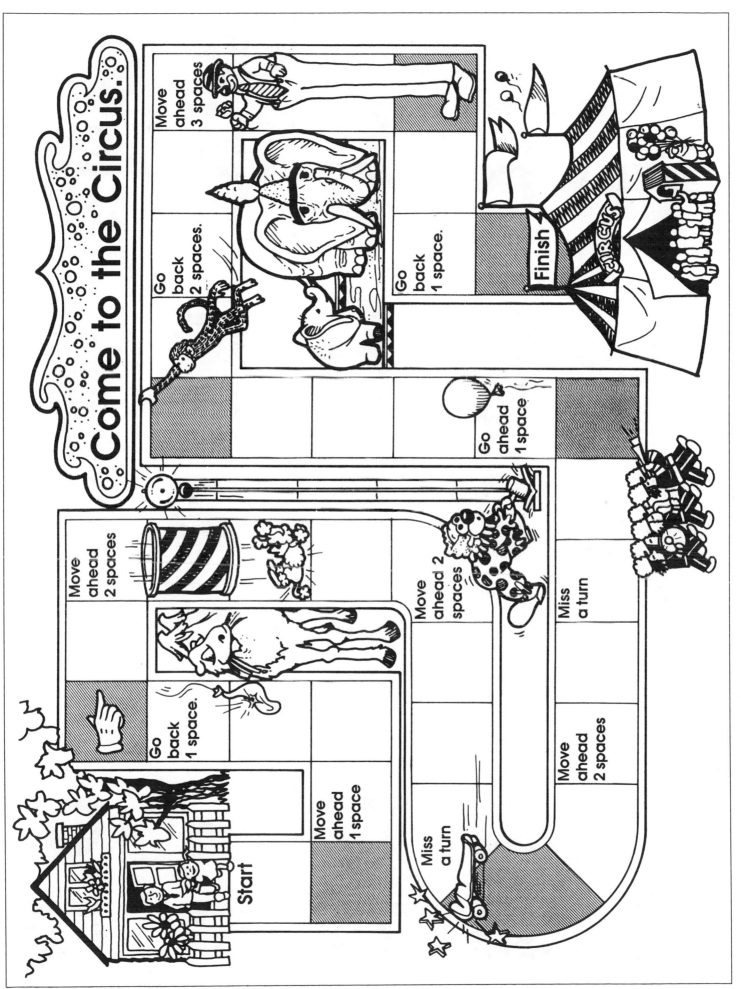

Come to the Circus.

Move ahead 3 spaces

Go back 2 spaces.

Go back 1 space.

Finish

CIRCUS

Go ahead 1 space

Move ahead 2 spaces

Move ahead 2 spaces

Miss a turn

Go back 1 space.

Move ahead 1 space

Miss a turn

Move ahead 2 spaces

Start

at	an	ap	en	et
bat	can	ap	gen	et
b	c	e	g	h
a	c	e	f	h
a	b	d	f	g
WORD CONSTRUCTION	b	d	e	g

ed	in	it	ig	op
ed	in	it	ig	op
j	l	m	o	p
j	k	m	o	p
i	k	l	n	p
i	j	l	n	o

ock	ot	un	up	ut
ock	ot	un	up	ut
s	t	v	x	z
r	t	v	x	z
r	s	u	w	y
q	s	u	w	y

Hello, _____ .

Hello, _____ .

To assemble, photocopy or staple page 178 back-to-back with page 177.

People like

Hello!

Hello!

by _____

© *date* _____

Hello, _____.

Hello, _____.

About the Book

Hello! is a book of greetings. On each page the author says hello to something or someone. The book is beautifully illustrated by the author.

About the Author

Author _____ is _____ years old. _____ lives in the city of _____.

Author

To assemble, photocopy or staple page 180 back-to-back with page 179.

can _____

. _____

Can!

by _____

© date _____

Praise for

Can!

can _____

. _____

·

ɔɐɔ

About the Book

You'll love reading **Can!** Discover four of the many things that are possible to do.

About the Author

Author _____ is ____ years old. The author can

_____ .

Author

eɐ (upside down "eat")

.

Here's what people are saying about
Eat!

eɐ (upside down "eat")

.

Eat!

by _____

© *date* _____

eat

eat

About the Book

Have you ever wondered what _____ eat? Read and discover four favorite foods of four fascinating creatures.

About the Author

Author _____ is _____ years old. _____ favorite food is _____.

Author

INDEX

MORE GOOD BOOKS FROM
WILLIAMSON PUBLISHING

To order additional copies of **Growing Up Reading**, please enclose $12.95 per copy plus $2.50 for shipping and handling. Follow "To Order" instructions on the last page. Thank you.

KIDS CREATE!
Art & Craft Experiences for 3– to 9–year–olds
by Laurie Carlson

What's the most important experience for children ages 3 to 9? Why, to create something by themselves. Carlson provides over 150 creative experiences ranging from making dinosaur sculptures to clay cactus gardens, from butterfly puppets to windsocks. Plenty of help for the parents working with the kids, too! A delightfully innovative book.

160 pages, 11 x 8½, over 400 illustrations
Quality paperback, $12.95

EcoArt!
Earth-Friendly Art & Craft Experiences for 3-to 9-year-olds
by Laurie Carlson

What better way to learn to love and care for the Earth than through creative art play! Laurie Carlson's latest book is packed with 150 projects using only recyclable, reusable, or nature's own found art materials. These fabulous activities are sure to please any child!

160 pages, 11 x 8½, 400 illustrations
Quality paperback, $12.95

THE KIDS' NATURE BOOK
365 Indoor/Outdoor Activities and Experiences
by Susan Milord

Winner of the Parents' Choice Gold Award for learning and doing books, *The Kids' Nature Book* is loved by children, grandparents, and friends alike. Simple projects and activities emphasize fun while quietly reinforcing the wonder of the world we all share. Packed with facts and fun!

160 pages, 11 x 8½, 425 illustrations
Quality paperback, $12.95

KIDS COOK!
Fabulous Food for the Whole Family
by Sarah Williamson and Zachary Williamson

Kids Cook! is filled with over 150 recipes for great tasting foods that kids ages 8 and up can cook for themselves and for their families and friends, too. Recipes from sections like "It's the Berries!" "Pasta Perfect,""Home Alone," "Side Orders," Babysitter's Bonanza," and "Best Bets for Brunch" include real, healthy foods — not cutesy recipes that are no fun to eat. Plus Nutri Notes, Safety First, and plenty of special menus for Father's Day, Grandma's Teatime, picnics, and parties. One terrific book!

160 pages, 11 x 8½, over 150 recipes, illustrations
Quality paperback, $12.95

DOING CHILDREN'S MUSEUMS
A Guide to 265 Hands-On Museums, Expanded and Updated
by Joanne Cleaver

Turn an ordinary day into a spontaneous "vacation" by taking a child to some of the 265 participatory children's museums, discovery rooms, and nature centers covered in this highly acclaimed, one-of-a-kind book. Filled with museum specifics to help you pick and plan the perfect place for the perfect day, Cleaver has created a most valuable resource for anyone who loves kids!

272 pages, 6 x 9
Quality paperback, $13.95

PARENTS ARE TEACHERS, TOO
Enriching Your Child's First Six Years
by Claudia Jones

Winner of the Parents' Choice Seal of Approval! Be the best teacher your child ever has. Jones shares hundreds of ways to help any child learn in playful home situations. Lots on developing reading, writing, math skills. Plenty on creative and critical thinking, too. A book you'll love using!

192 pages, 6 x 9, illustrations
Quality paperback, $9.95

<u>MORE</u> PARENTS ARE TEACHERS, TOO
Encouraging Your 6- to 12-Year-Old
by Claudia Jones

Winner of the Parents' Choice Seal of Approval! Help your children be the best they can be! When parents are involved, kids do better. When kids do better, they feel better, too. Here's a wonderfully creative book of ideas, activities, teaching methods and more to help you help your children over the rough spots and share in their growing joy in achieving. Plenty on reading, writing, math, problem-solving, creative thinking. Everything for parents who want to help but not push their children.

224 pages, 6 x 9, illustrations
Quality paperback, $10.95

HANDS AROUND THE WORLD
365 Creative Ways to Build Cultural Awareness & Global Respect
by Susan Milord

The latest book by award-winning author Susan Milord invites children to experience, taste, and embrace the daily lives of children from the far corners of the earth. In 365 days of experiences, it tears down stereotypes and replaces them with the fascinating realities of our differences and our similarities. Children everywhere can plant and grow, write and tell stories, draw and craft, cook and eat, sing and dance, look and explore, as they learn to live in an atmosphere of global respect and cultural awareness that is born of personal experience.

160 pages, 11 x 8½, over 400 illustrations
Quality paperback, $12.95

THE KIDS' MULTICULTURAL ART BOOK
Art & Craft Experiences from Around the World
by Alexandra M. Terzian

Alexandra Terzian brings an unsurpassed enthusiasm to the hands-on multicultural art experience. Children will reach across continents and oceans with paper, paste, and paints, while absorbing basic sensibilities about the wondrous cultures of others. Children will learn by making such things as the *Korhogo Mud Cloth* and the *Wodaabe Mirror Pouch* from Africa, the *Chippawa Dream Catcher* of the American Indian, the *Kokeshi Doll* of Japan, the *Chinese Opera Mask*, the *Mexican Folk Art Tree of Life*, the *Twirling Palm Puppet* from India, and the *Guatemalan Green Toad Bank*. A virtual feast of multicultural art and craft experiences!

160 pages, 11 x 8½, over 400 how-to-do-it illustrations
Quality paperback, $12.95

KIDS LEARN AMERICA!
Bringing Geography to Life with People, Places, & History
by Patricia Gordon and Reed C. Snow

Designed to help increase "geo-literacy," Kids Learn America! is not about memorizing. This creative and exciting new book is about making every region of our country come alive from within, about being connected to the earth and the people across this great expanse called America. ☆ Activities and games targeted to the 50 states plus D.C. and Puerto Rico ☆ The environment and natural resources ☆ Geographic comparisons ☆ Fascinating facts, famous people and places of each region. Let us all join together — kids, parents, friends, teachers, grandparents — and put America, its geography, its history, and its heritage back on the map!

176 pages, 11 x 8½, maps, illustrations
Quality paperback, $12.95

KIDS & WEEKENDS!
Creative Ways to Make Special Days
by Avery Hart and Paul Mantell

Packed with truly creative ways to play, have fun, learn, grow, and build self-esteem and positive relationships, this book is a must for every parent, grandparent, baby-sitter, and teacher. Hart and Mantell will inspire us all to transform some part of every weekend — even if it is only 30 minutes — into a special experience. Everything from backyard nature to putting on a magic show to creating a bird sanctuary to writing a book about yourself to environmentally sound activities indoors and out. Whatever your interests, no matter how busy you are, kids and their families will savor special weekend moments.

176 pages, 11 x 8½, over 400 illustrations
Quality paperback, $12.95

ADVENTURES IN ART
Art & Craft Experiences for 7- to 14-year-olds
by Susan Milord

Imagine an art book that encourages children to explore, to experience, to touch and to see, to learn and to create . . . imagine a true adventure in art. Here's a book that teaches artisans' skills without stifling creativity. Covers making handmade papers, puppets, masks, paper seascapes, seed art, tin can lantern, berry ink, still life, silk screen, batiking, carving, and so much more. Perfect for the older child. Let the adventure begin!

160 pages, 11 x 8½, 500 illustrations
Quality paperback, $12.95

KIDS MAKE MUSIC!
Clapping and Tapping from Bach to Rock
by Avery Hart and Paul Mantell

No instruments necessary — just hands, feet, and wiggly bodies! Kids are natural music makers, and with the kid-loving music makers, Avery Hart and Paul Mantell, children everywhere will be doing the *Dinosaur Dance*, singing the *Dishwashin' Blues*, cleaning their rooms to Rap, belting it out in a *Jug Band* or *An Accidental Orchestra*, putting on a *Fairy Tale Opera*, learning to *Tap Dance* or creating a *Bona Fide Ballet* (homemade tutu included)! Those hands will be clapping, those feet will be tapping, those faces will be grinning, and they may be humming anything from Bach to Rock.

160 pages, 11 x 8½, with hundreds of illustrations
Quality paperback, $12.95

THE HOMEWORK SOLUTION
by Linda Agler Sonna

Put homework responsibilities where they belong — in the student's lap! Here it is! The simple remedy for the millions of parents who are tired of waging the never-ending nightly battle over kids' homework. Dr. Sonna's "One Step Solution" will relieve parents, kids, and their siblings of the ongoing problem within a single month.

192 pages, 6 x 9
Quality paperback, $10.95

THE BROWN BAG COOKBOOK
Nutritious Portable Lunches for Kids and Grown-Ups
by Sara Sloan

Now in its ninth printing this popular book has more than 1,000 brown bag lunch ideas with 150 recipes for simple, quick, nutritious lunches that kids will love. Breakfast ideas, too! The more people care what they eat, the more popular this book becomes.

192 pages, $8\frac{1}{4}$ x $7\frac{1}{4}$, illustrations
Quality paperback, $9.95

SUGAR-FREE TODDLERS
by Susan Watson

Here are over 100 recipes for nution-filled breakfasts, lunches, snacks, beverages, and more. And best of all, they're all sugar-free. Plus ratings for hundreds of store-bought products, too. If you have young children, they need you to have this book.

160 pages, $8\frac{1}{4}$ x $7\frac{1}{4}$, 150 illustrations
Quality paperback, $9.95

To Order:

At your bookstore or order directly from Williamson Publishing. We accept Visa and MasterCard (please include number and expiration date), or send check to:

Williamson Publishing Company
Church Hill Road, P.O. Box 185
Charlotte, Vermont 05445

Toll-free phone orders with credit cards:
1-800-234-8791

Please add $2.50 for postage and handling. Satisfaction is guaranteed or full refund without questions or quibbles.

JAN 1994